Best-Ever Recipes

Published by John Wiley & Sons, Inc., Hoboken, New Jersey

This edition is published in arrangement with ACP Magazines Ltd, Australia and is derived from copyright works originally published in Australia by ACP Magazines Ltd. ACP Magazines Ltd is either the copyright owner or licensee of the content contained in this edition and reserves all rights.

For general information on our other products and services or for technical support, please contact our Customer Care Department within the United States at (800) 762–2974, outside the United States at (317) 572–3993 or fax (317) 572–4002.

Wiley also publishes its books in a variety of electronic formats. Some content that appears in print may not be available in electronic books. For more information about Wiley products, visit our web site at www.wiley.com.

Library of Congress Cataloging-in-Publication Data:

Best-ever recipes / by ACP Books.

    p. cm.

 Includes index.

 ISBN 978-0-470-44054-4 (pbk.)

1. Cookery. 2. Cookery, International. I. ACP Books. II. ACP magazines LTD.

 TX714.B3993 2009

 641.59--dc22

Printed in the United States of America

10 9 8 7 6 5 4 3 2 1

In this collection of best-ever recipes, you'll find time-tested classics, fresh new favorites from restaurant menus, and popular ethnic dishes from the simple to the spectacular. From appetizers to desserts, this book is an essential resource for today's home cook.

Contents

Soups & Salads

The most casual and comforting of foods, soups and salads are quite versatile. They make great starters, but can also be served as a main course for lunch, a relaxed family dinner, or feed a crowd.

roasted garlic and potato soup

preparation time 10 minutes **cooking time** 30 minutes **serves** 4

2 medium garlic bulbs, unpeeled

2 tablespoons olive oil

2 medium yellow onions, chopped coarsely

1 tablespoon fresh thyme leaves

5 medium potatoes (about 2 pounds),
   cut into bite-sized pieces

5 cups chicken stock

¾ cup heavy cream

1 Preheat oven to 375°F.

2 Separate garlic bulbs into cloves; place unpeeled cloves, in single layer, on baking sheet. Drizzle with half of the oil. Roast, uncovered, about 15 minutes or until garlic is soft. Remove from oven; when cool enough to handle, squeeze garlic into small bowl, discarding the skins.

3 Heat remaining oil in large pot; cook onion and thyme, stirring, until onion softens. Add potato; cook, stirring, 5 minutes. Add stock; bring to a boil. Reduce heat; simmer, uncovered, about 15 minutes or until potato is just tender. Stir in garlic; simmer, uncovered, 5 minutes.

4 Blend or process soup (or pass through a food mill or fine sieve), in batches, until smooth, then return to pan. Reheat until hot, then stir in cream. Divide soup among serving bowls; sprinkle with extra thyme, if desired.

Tip Garlic's cooking times make a huge difference to its pungency: the longer it's cooked, the more creamy in texture and subtly nutty in flavor it becomes.

NUTRITIONAL INFO PER SERVING 28g total fat (13g saturated fat); 37g carbohydrate; 12g protein; 9g fiber; 446 calories

minestrone

preparation time 40 minutes (plus refrigeration times) **cooking time** 3 hours 15 minutes **serves** 6

There are as many versions of minestrone as there are regions in Italy. This recipe is based on a seasonal soup made in Milan, where the cold winters seem to inspire hearty fare like this. Rice, rather than pasta is used as a thickener, and the ham hocks impart a pleasing smoky flavor that seems to fight the chill.

2 ham hocks (2 pounds)
1 medium onion, chopped coarsely
1 celery stalk, chopped coarsely
1 teaspoon black peppercorns
1 bay leaf
4 large carrots, chopped coarsely
4 quarts (16 cups) water
1 ½ tablespoons olive oil
1 large white onion, chopped coarsely
3 cloves garlic, crushed
14 ½-ounce can cannellini or
　 Great Northern beans, drained
4 small tomatoes, peeled,
　 chopped coarsely
1 ½ tablespoons tomato paste
2 celery stalks, chopped coarsely
2 medium potatoes, chopped coarsely
½ small cabbage (about 1 ¼ pounds),
　 shredded coarsely
2 medium zucchini, chopped coarsely
½ cup arborio rice
¼ cup finely chopped fresh flat-leaf parsley
3 tablespoons finely shredded fresh basil

1 Preheat oven to 425°F; roast ham hocks and onion on baking sheet, uncovered, 30 minutes. Combine ham hocks and onion with celery, peppercorns, bay leaf, a third of the carrots and the water in large pot; bring to a boil. Reduce heat; simmer, uncovered, 2 hours. Strain stock through cheesecloth-lined sieve or colander into large bowl; discard solids. Allow stock to cool, cover; refrigerate until cold. (Can be made ahead to this stage. Cover; refrigerate overnight.)
2 Heat oil in large pot; cook onion and garlic, stirring, until onion softens. Discard fat from surface of stock. Add stock, beans and tomatoes to pot with tomato paste, celery, potatoes and remaining carrots; bring to a boil. Reduce heat; simmer, covered, about 20 minutes.
3 Add cabbage, zucchini and rice; simmer, uncovered, about 15 minutes or until rice is just tender. Stir in parsley and basil just before serving.

Tip You can substitute a small short pasta such as elbow macaroni for the rice if you prefer; add it with the cabbage and zucchini, but cook it only until tender.

NUTRITIONAL INFO PER SERVING 6g total fat (1g saturated fat); 38g carbohydrate; 16g protein; 11g fiber; 285 calories

French onion soup

preparation time 30 minutes **cooking time** 50 minutes **serves** 4

4 tablespoons butter

4 large onions (about 1 ¾ pounds),
   halved, sliced thinly

¾ cup dry white wine

3 cups water

1 quart (4 cups) beef stock

1 bay leaf

1 ½ tablespoons all-purpose flour

1 teaspoon fresh thyme

1 small French baguette

1 cup finely grated gruyère cheese

1 Melt butter in large pot; cook onions, stirring occasionally, over medium heat, about 30 minutes or until caramelized.

2 Bring wine to a boil in medium pot; boil 1 minute. Stir in the water, stock and bay leaf; return to a boil. Remove from heat.

3 Stir flour into onion mixture; cook, stirring, until mixture bubbles and thickens. Gradually add hot stock mixture, stirring until mixture boils and thickens slightly. Reduce heat; simmer soup, uncovered, stirring occasionally, 20 minutes. Discard bay leaf; stir in thyme.

4 Cut bread into ½-inch slices. Toast slices on one side under preheated broiler. Turn slices; top each with about 1 ½ tablespoons of the cheese; broil croutons until cheese melts.

5 Divide soup among bowls; top with croutons, sprinkle with remaining cheese.

NUTRITIONAL INFO PER SERVING 21g total fat (13g saturated fat); 29g carbohydrate; 18g protein; 4g fiber; 411 calories

white bean sausage soup

preparation time 30 minutes **cooking time** 35 minutes **serves** 6

Pistou, from the south of France (similar to Italian pesto) is delicious stirred into soups.

3 tablespoons butter

2 slices bacon (5 ounces), chopped finely

2 cloves garlic, crushed

1 medium leek, sliced thinly

2 celery stalks, chopped finely

3 large carrots, chopped finely

1 ½ quarts (6 cups) chicken stock

1 bay leaf

14 ½-ounce can cannellini or
    Great Northern beans, drained

11 ounces Italian sausages

Pistou

2 cups loosely packed fresh basil

1 clove garlic, quartered

¼ cup coarsely grated parmesan cheese

¼ cup extra virgin olive oil

1 Melt butter in large pot; cook bacon, garlic, leek, celery and carrots, stirring, until vegetables soften. Stir in stock, bay leaf and beans; bring to a boil. Reduce heat; simmer soup, covered, about 20 minutes.

2 Make pistou.

3 Heat medium non-stick skillet; cook sausages until browned. Drain on paper towels; chop coarsely.

4 Just before serving, ladle soup into serving bowls; top with sausages and a spoonful of pistou.

Pistou Blend or process ingredients until smooth

NUTRITIONAL INFO PER SERVING 32g total fat (13g saturated fat); 11g carbohydrate; 16g protein; 6g fiber; 407 calories

Cuban black bean soup

preparation time 30 minutes (plus standing time) **cooking time** 2 hours 15 minutes **serves** 8

Ask your butcher to cut the ham bone in half for you so it fits more easily into the pot.

2 ½ cups dried black beans

2-pound ham bone

¼ cup olive oil

2 medium onions, chopped finely

1 medium red bell pepper, chopped finely

4 cloves garlic, crushed

1 ½ tablespoons ground cumin

1 teaspoon crushed red pepper flakes

14-ounce can chopped tomatoes,
  undrained

2 ½ quarts (10 cups) water

1 ½ tablespoons dried oregano

2 teaspoons ground black pepper

¼ cup fresh lime juice

2 medium tomatoes, chopped finely

¼ cup coarsely chopped fresh cilantro

1 Place beans in medium bowl, cover with water; let stand overnight, drain. Rinse under cold water; drain.

2 Preheat oven to 425°F; roast ham bone on baking sheet, uncovered, 30 minutes.

3 Heat oil in large pot; cook onions, bell pepper and garlic, stirring, about 5 minutes or until vegetables soften. Add cumin and chili; cook, stirring, 1 minute. Add beans and ham bone to pot with tomatoes, the water, oregano and pepper; bring to a boil. Reduce heat; simmer, uncovered, 1 ½ hours. (Can be made ahead to this stage. Cover; refrigerate overnight.)

4 Remove ham bone from soup; shred ham from bone. Discard bone; add ham to soup, stirring until heated through. Stir lime juice, tomatoes and cilantro into soup just before serving.

Tip Some Cuban recipes call for half of the beans to be mashed then returned to the soup, giving it a smoother, velvety texture.

NUTRITIONAL INFO PER SERVING 9g total fat (1g saturated fat); 27g carbohydrate; 17g protein; 14g fiber; 208 calories

soup with pistou

preparation time 15 minutes **cooking time** 1 hour 40 minutes **serves** 8

Soup with pistou is a classic Provençale recipe, which benefits from being made a day in advance.

⅓ cup olive oil

2 veal shanks (3 ½ pounds), trimmed

1 large leek (about 1 pound), sliced thinly

2 quarts (8 cups) water

2 cups chicken stock

3 tablespoons toasted pine nuts

1 clove garlic, quartered

¼ cup finely grated parmesan cheese

½ cup firmly packed fresh basil

14 ½-ounce can cannellini or
    Great Northern beans, drained

3 large carrots, chopped coarsely

7 ounces green beans, trimmed,
    chopped coarsely

1 Heat 1 ½ tablespoons of the oil in large pot; cook shanks, uncovered, until browned all over. Remove from pot. Cook leek in same pot, stirring, 5 minutes or until just softened. Return shanks to pot with the water and stock; bring to a boil. Reduce heat; simmer, covered, 1 hour.

2 Blend or process remaining oil, nuts, garlic and cheese until combined. Add basil; process until pistou mixture forms a paste.

3 Remove shanks from soup. When cool enough to handle, remove meat from bones. Discard bones; chop meat coarsely. Return meat to soup with cannellini beans; bring to a boil. Reduce heat; simmer, uncovered, 20 minutes. Add carrots; simmer, uncovered, 10 minutes. Add green beans and pistou; simmer, uncovered, 5 minutes.

4 Divide soup among serving bowls. Serve with warm bread, if desired.

NUTRITIONAL INFO PER SERVING 14g total fat (2g saturated fat); 8g carbohydrate; 30g protein; 5g fiber; 281 calories

grilled tomato and red pepper gazpacho

preparation time 30 minutes **cooking time** 25 minutes (plus refrigeration time) **serves** 4

3 medium red bell peppers (1 ¼ pounds)

6 medium plum tomatoes (1 pound),
  halved, seeded

1 medium red onion, sliced thickly

4 cloves garlic, unpeeled

2 cucumbers, seeded, chopped coarsely

3 tablespoons red wine vinegar

14-ounce can tomato juice

1 ½ tablespoons coarsely chopped
  fresh flat-leaf parsley

¼ cup cold water

Parmesan croutons

1 ½ tablespoons butter, melted

1 ½ tablespoons olive oil

1 ½ tablespoons finely grated
  parmesan cheese

3 slices white bread, crusts removed,
  quartered

1 Quarter bell peppers, discard seeds and membranes. Roast under broiler or in an oven preheated to 475°F, skin-side up, until skin blisters and blackens. Cover bell pepper in plastic wrap or aluminum foil for 5 minutes; peel away skin, chop coarsely.

2 Cook tomatoes, onion and garlic on heated oiled grill pan until tender. When cool enough to handle, peel garlic.

3 Blend or process bell peppers, tomatoes, onion, garlic, cucumber, vinegar, tomato juice and parsley, in batches, until gazpacho is smooth. Transfer to large bowl, cover; refrigerate about 3 hours or until cold.

4 Make parmesan croutons.

5 Stir cold water into gazpacho. Serve chilled gazpacho sprinkled with croutons and extra chopped parsley.

Parmesan croutons Combine butter, oil and cheese in small bowl; add bread, turn to coat in mixture. Cook croutons on heated oiled grill pan until browned on both sides.

NUTRITIONAL INFO PER SERVING 11g total fat (4g saturated fat); 32g carbohydrate; 9g protein; 7g fiber; 477 calories

California salad

preparation time 20 minutes **cooking time** 5 minutes **serves** 4

8 ounces sugar snap peas, trimmed

1 large apple (Granny Smith)

1 pound lump crabmeat, drained

1 medium red onion, halved, sliced thinly

2 fresh small red serrano or jalapeño peppers, seeded, sliced thinly lengthwise (optional)

2 medium avocados, sliced into thick pieces

6 ounces mixed salad greens

⅓ cup olive oil

¼ cup fresh lemon juice

1 tablespoon Dijon mustard

1 clove garlic, crushed

1 Boil, steam, or microwave peas until tender; drain. Rinse under cold water; drain.

2 Cut apple into thin slices; cut slices into thin strips. Combine peas and apple in large bowl with crab, onion, pepper, avocados, and salad greens.

3 Place remaining ingredients in screw-top jar; shake well. Drizzle dressing over salad; toss gently to combine.

NUTRITIONAL INFO PER SERVING 39g total fat (7g saturated fat); 12g carbohydrate; 21g protein; 5g fiber; 492 calories

Mediterranean chicken salad

preparation time 30 minutes **cooking time** 25 minutes **serves** 4

1 ½ cups chicken stock

½ cup dry white wine

4 boneless, skinless chicken breasts
  (1 ½ pounds)

2 medium yellow bell peppers

1 large loaf sourdough bread

7 tablespoons butter, melted

2 cloves garlic, crushed

1 ½ tablespoons finely chopped
  fresh flat-leaf parsley

5 cups baby arugula leaves

8 ounces grape or cherry tomatoes,
  halved

⅓ cup pitted black olives

Anchovy dressing

½ cup firmly packed fresh basil

½ cup extra virgin olive oil

3 tablespoons finely grated
  parmesan cheese

2 drained anchovy fillets

1 ½ tablespoons fresh lemon juice

1 Bring stock and wine to a boil in large skillet. Add chicken, reduce heat; simmer, covered, about 8 minutes or until cooked through, turning once halfway through cooking time. Let chicken stand in stock for 10 minutes; slice chicken thinly, reserve stock for another use, if desired.

2 Quarter bell peppers; remove and discard seeds and membranes. Roast under broiler or at 475°F, skin-side up, until skin blisters and blackens. Cover bell pepper pieces with plastic wrap or aluminum foil for 5 minutes. Peel away skin; slice bell pepper thinly.

3 Preheat oven to 400°F (or reduce oven temperature to 400°F).

4 Cut bread into ¾-inch slices; remove and discard crusts, cut slices into 1 ¼-inch cubes. Toss bread in large bowl with combined butter, garlic and parsley; spread bread, in single layer, over two baking sheets. Toast in oven about 10 minutes or until croutons are crisp and lightly browned.

5 Make anchovy dressing.

6 Place chicken, bell pepper and croutons in large bowl with arugula, tomatoes, olives and dressing; toss gently to combine.

Anchovy dressing Blend or process ingredients until smooth.

Tip Chicken and croutons can be made a day ahead.

NUTRITIONAL INFO PER SERVING 64g total fat (22g saturated fat); 64g carbohydrate; 53g protein; 9g fiber; 1075 calories

avocado caprese salad

preparation time 10 minutes **serves** 4

Try to find buffalo mozzarella — it's made from buffalo's milk and has a creamier texture than regular mozzarella.

4 large heirloom or vine-ripened tomatoes (about 1 pound)
½ pound fresh mozzarella cheese
1 large avocado (about ¾ pound), halved
¼ cup loosely packed fresh basil leaves
2 tablespoons olive oil
1 tablespoon balsamic vinegar

1 Slice tomato, cheese and avocado thickly.
2 Place slices of tomato, cheese and avocado on serving platter; top with basil leaves, drizzle with combined oil and vinegar. Sprinkle with freshly ground black pepper.

Tip With a simple recipe like this, use the most flavorful tomatoes you can find.

NUTRITIONAL INFO PER SERVING 29g total fat (10g saturated fat); 2g carbohydrate; 13g protein; 2g fiber; 321 calories

Caesar salad

preparation time 30 minutes **cooking time** 20 minutes **serves** 4

½ loaf crusty Italian bread
1 clove garlic, crushed
⅓ cup olive oil
2 eggs
1 large or 3 small heads Romaine lettuce
    (about 1 pound), leaves separated
1 cup shaved parmesan cheese

Caesar dressing
1 clove garlic, crushed
1 tablespoon Dijon mustard
3 tablespoons fresh lemon juice
2 teaspoons Worcestershire sauce
3 tablespoons olive oil

1 Preheat oven to 350°F.
2 Cut bread into ¾-inch cubes. Combine garlic and oil in large bowl, add bread; toss bread to coat in oil mixture. Place bread, in single layer, on baking sheets; toast, uncovered, about 15 minutes or until croutons are browned lightly.
3 Bring water to a boil in small pot; using slotted spoon, carefully lower whole eggs into water. Cover pot tightly, remove from heat; using same slotted spoon, remove eggs from water after 1 minute. When cool enough to handle, break eggs into large bowl, add lettuce; toss gently to combine. Add cheese and croutons.
4 Make Caesar dressing.
5 Pour dressing over salad; toss gently to combine. Divide among serving plates; sprinkle with freshly ground black pepper, if desired.
Caesar dressing Whisk together ingredients.

NUTRITIONAL INFO PER SERVING 38g total fat (9g saturated fat); 28g carbohydrate; 18g protein; 5g fiber; 525 calories

composed salad

preparation time 15 minutes **cooking time** 20 minutes **serves** 4

The ingredients in this dish are layered on top of each other, rather than tossed together, and the dressing is drizzled over the top.

1 small French baguette

2 cloves garlic, crushed

¼ cup olive oil

10 slices bacon (15 ounces),
   sliced thickly

3 cups mixed salad greens

6 medium plum tomatoes
   (about 1 pound), sliced thinly

4 hard-boiled eggs, halved lengthwise

Red wine vinaigrette

¼ cup red wine vinegar

3 teaspoons Dijon mustard

⅓ cup extra virgin olive oil

1 Preheat broiler.

2 Cut bread into ½-inch slices. Brush both sides with combined garlic and oil; toast under broiler.

3 Cook bacon in large skillet until crisp; drain on paper towels.

4 Make red wine vinaigrette.

5 Layer bread and bacon in large bowl with salad greens and tomatoes, top with eggs; drizzle with vinaigrette.

Red wine vinaigrette Whisk together ingredients.

NUTRITIONAL INFO PER SERVING 48g total fat (10g saturated fat); 20g carbohydrate; 25g protein; 4g fiber; 616 calories

warm goat cheese and lentil salad

preparation time 40 minutes **cooking time** 30 minutes **serves** 4

1 medium red bell pepper, sliced thickly

3 tablespoons extra virgin olive oil

½ cup lentils, rinsed, drained

1 medium onion, halved

1 bay leaf

16 sprigs fresh thyme

10 ½-ounce piece firm goat cheese

3 tablespoons dried breadcrumbs

2 teaspoons finely grated lemon peel

1 ½ tablespoons coarsely chopped
    fresh flat-leaf parsley

8 ounces cherry tomatoes, halved

2 cups mixed salad greens

Vinaigrette

1 ½ tablespoons red wine vinegar

3 tablespoons extra virgin olive oil

1 teaspoon Dijon mustard

1 teaspoon sugar

1 Preheat oven to 425°F.

2 Combine bell pepper and half of the oil in large shallow baking dish; toss to coat bell pepper. Roast, uncovered, about 15 minutes or until bell pepper softens.

3 Combine lentils, onion, bay leaf and thyme in medium pot, cover with water; bring to a boil. Reduce heat; simmer, covered, about 20 minutes or until lentils are just tender. Drain; discard onion, bay leaf and thyme.

4 Make vinaigrette.

5 Cut cheese into 16 pieces; coat cheese in breadcrumbs. Heat remaining oil in medium skillet; cook cheese, uncovered, about 5 minutes or until cheese is browned lightly all over and starting to melt.

6 Combine lentils in medium bowl with lemon peel, parsley, tomatoes and two-thirds of the vinaigrette. Divide lentils among serving plates; top with bell pepper, salad greens, cheese and drizzle with remaining vinaigrette.

Vinaigrette Whisk together ingredients.

NUTRITIONAL INFO PER SERVING 31g total fat (10g saturated fat); 11g carbohydrate; 13g protein; 3g fiber; 373 calories

grilled radicchio and roasted tomato salad

preparation time 10 minutes **cooking time** 20 minutes **serves** 6

⅓ cup olive oil

1 clove garlic, crushed

6 medium plum tomatoes
(about 1 pound), halved

4 small heads radicchio
(about 1 ¼ pounds), quartered

3 tablespoons balsamic vinegar

3 ½ cups baby arugula leaves

⅔ cup shaved romano or parmesan cheese

1 Preheat oven to 425°F.

2 Combine 1 ½ tablespoons of the oil with garlic in small bowl. Place tomatoes, cut-side up, on baking sheet; drizzle with oil mixture. Roast, uncovered, about 20 minutes or until softened.

3 Combine radicchio with 3 tablespoons of the remaining oil in large bowl. Cook radicchio on heated oiled grill pan (or grill) until browned all over; cool 5 minutes.

4 Whisk together vinegar and remaining oil. Arrange tomatoes, radicchio and arugula on large serving platter; sprinkle with cheese, drizzle with dressing.

NUTRITIONAL INFO PER SERVING 15g total fat (3g saturated fat); 3g carbohydrate; 5g protein; 3g fiber; 163 calories

Appetizers

For many people, appetizers are the best part of the meal. These savory small bites are usually intensely flavored, and leave you wanting more.

olive and tomato bruschetta

preparation time 25 minutes **cooking time** 5 minutes **makes** 20

1-pound loaf crusty Italian bread
⅓ cup extra virgin olive oil
1 cup seeded Kalamata olives, chopped coarsely
1 cup stuffed green olives, chopped coarsely
1 cup coarsely chopped drained sun-dried tomatoes
1 ½ tablespoons drained baby capers, rinsed
2 drained anchovy fillets, chopped finely
¼ cup finely shredded fresh basil
1 clove garlic, crushed
3 tablespoons red wine vinegar

1 Preheat broiler.

2 Cut bread into ½-inch slices; brush with ¼ cup of the oil. Toast bread under broiler on both sides.

3 Combine remaining oil and remaining ingredients in medium bowl.

4 Place bread on serving plates; top with olive mixture.

Tip Olive mixture can be made a day ahead and kept covered in the refrigerator.

NUTRITIONAL INFO PER BRUSCHETTA 6g total fat (1g saturated fat); 14g carbohydrate; 3g protein; 2g fiber; 119 calories

Italian stuffed mushrooms

preparation time 15 minutes **cooking time** 15 minutes **serves** 4

Marsala is a sweet fortified wine originally from Sicily; it can be found in most grocery or liquor stores.

8 medium portabella mushrooms
　(1 ¾ pounds)
6 ½ tablespoons butter
½ medium red bell pepper, chopped finely
1 clove garlic, crushed
¼ cup marsala wine
1 ½ tablespoons fresh lemon juice
1 ½ cups stale breadcrumbs
3 tablespoons coarsely chopped fresh
　flat-leaf parsley
1 cup coarsely grated pecorino cheese

1 Preheat oven to 400°F.

2 Carefully remove stems from mushrooms; chop stems finely.

3 Melt butter in small skillet. Brush mushroom caps with about half of the butter; place on greased baking sheets.

4 Cook bell pepper and garlic, stirring in remaining butter until bell pepper is tender. Add chopped mushroom stems, marsala, lemon juice and breadcrumbs; cook, stirring, 3 minutes. Remove from heat; stir in parsley and cheese.

5 Spoon filling into mushroom caps; bake, uncovered, about 10 minutes or until browned.

Tip Vegetable stock or chicken stock can be substituted for marsala, if desired.

NUTRITIONAL INFO PER SERVING 26g total fat (16g saturated fat); 20g carbohydrate; 17g protein; 7g fiber; 398 calories

caramelized onion and goat cheese tartlets

preparation time 25 minutes (plus refrigeration time) **cooking time** 45 minutes **serves** 4

1 cup all-purpose flour

6 tablespoons cold butter, chopped

1 egg yolk

3 tablespoons cold water

3 ½ ounces goat cheese

3 tablespoons coarsely chopped
   fresh chives

Caramelized onions

3 tablespoons olive oil

4 large onions (about 1 ¾ pounds),
   sliced thinly

⅓ cup port

3 tablespoons red wine vinegar

3 tablespoons brown sugar

1 Blend or process flour and butter until mixture is crumbly. Add egg yolk and the water; process until ingredients come together. Cover with plastic wrap; refrigerate 30 minutes.

2 Make caramelized onions.

3 Preheat oven to 400°F. Grease four 4 ½-inch tart pans with removable bases.

4 Divide pastry into four portions. Roll one portion of pastry between sheets of parchment paper until large enough to line pan. Lift pastry into pan; press into sides, trim edges, prick crust all over with fork. Repeat with remaining pastry.

5 Place pans on baking sheet; cover crusts with parchment paper, fill with dried beans or rice. Bake, uncovered, 10 minutes. Remove paper and beans carefully; bake additional 5 minutes or until crusts brown lightly.

6 Divide onion mixture and cheese among tartlets. Bake, uncovered, about 5 minutes or until heated through. Sprinkle with chives.

Caramelized onions Heat oil in large skillet; cook onions, stirring, until onions soften. Add port, vinegar and sugar; cook, stirring occasionally, about 25 minutes or until onions caramelize.

NUTRITIONAL INFO PER SERVING 32g total fat (15g saturated fat); 44g carbohydrate; 11g protein; 4g fiber; 518 calories

smoked salmon with avocado salsa and shrimp

preparation time 35 minutes **serves** 8

24 slices smoked salmon (14 ounces)
16 cooked large shrimp (1 ½ pounds)
1 ½ tablespoons salmon roe (optional)
8 fresh dill sprigs

Avocado salsa

2 medium plum tomatoes, seeded,
 chopped finely
2 small avocados, chopped finely
½ small red onion, chopped finely
1 ½ tablespoons finely chopped
 fresh chives
2 teaspoons finely chopped fresh dill
1 teaspoon finely grated lemon peel
3 tablespoons lemon juice

Lemon chive dressing

¼ cup olive oil
3 tablespoons lemon juice
1 ½ tablespoons finely chopped
 fresh chives

1 Make avocado salsa.

2 Line eight cups of a 12-cup muffin pan with plastic wrap, bringing the plastic 1 ¼ inches above the edges of each cup. Place one salmon slice in base of each cup and fold over excess. Top each slice with 3 tablespoons of the salsa; lay another slice of salmon in each cup. Top each with another 3 tablespoons of the salsa; lay another slice of salmon in each cup. Fold over plastic to seal; refrigerate until needed.

3 Peel and devein shrimp, leaving tails intact.

4 Make lemon chive dressing.

5 Turn out and unwrap salmon packages. Divide packages among serving plates; top with shrimp, roe and dill, drizzle with dressing.

Avocado salsa Combine ingredients in small bowl.

Lemon chive dressing Whisk together ingredients in small bowl.

NUTRITIONAL INFO PER SERVING 18g total fat (3g saturated fat); 1g carbohydrate; 24g protein; 1g fiber; 259 calories

tuna tartare on wonton chips

preparation time 20 minutes **cooking time** 10 minutes **makes** 24

3 ½ ounces sashimi-grade tuna,
  chopped finely

½ small red onion, chopped finely

1 ½ tablespoons finely chopped fresh mint

1 ½ tablespoons finely chopped
  fresh cilantro

1 ½ tablespoons fresh lime juice

1 ½ tablespoons fish sauce

six 3-inch square wonton wrappers

vegetable oil, for deep-frying

24 fresh baby cilantro leaves

1 Combine tuna, onion, mint, cilantro, lime juice and fish sauce in small bowl.

2 Cut each wrapper into four triangles. Heat oil in wok; deep-fry triangles, in batches, until crisp. Drain on paper towels.

3 Place triangles on serving platter; top with a heaping teaspoon of tuna mixture and one cilantro leaf.

NUTRITIONAL INFO PER WONTON CHIP 1g total fat (0g saturated fat); 1g carbohydrate; 1g protein; 0g fiber; 14 calories

potato pancakes with smoked salmon

preparation time 20 minutes **cooking time** 20 minutes **serves** 4

Pan-fried potato cakes are best made from a starchy potato variety, such as russet or Idaho.

4 medium potatoes (about 1¾ pounds),
  (peeled, if desired)
3 tablespoons vegetable oil
½ cup (4 ounces) spreadable light
  cream cheese
1 ½ tablespoons finely chopped fresh
  flat-leaf parsley
1 ½ tablespoons finely chopped
  fresh chives
1 ½ tablespoons fresh lemon juice
5 ounces sliced smoked salmon

1 Coarsely grate potatoes; use hands to squeeze out as much excess liquid as possible. Measure ¼ cups of grated potatoes, placing each portion on long sheet of parchment paper.

2 Heat 2 teaspoons of the oil in large non-stick skillet; place two portions of the grated potatoes in skillet, flattening each with spatula. Cook patties over medium heat until browned; turn with spatula to cook other side. Drain patties on paper towels; make six more potato cakes with remaining oil and grated potatoes.

3 Combine cream cheese, herbs and lemon juice in small bowl.

4 Divide potato pancakes among four serving plates, top with herbed cream cheese and smoked salmon.

NUTRITIONAL INFO PER SERVING 16g total fat (5g saturated fat);
24g carbohydrate; 15g protein; 3g fiber; 307 calories

chicken quesadillas with guacamole

preparation time 15 minutes **cooking time** 30 minutes **serves** 4

1 ½ tablespoons olive oil

2 cloves garlic, crushed

1 small red onion, chopped finely

¼ teaspoon cayenne pepper

2 teaspoons ground cumin

1 medium red bell pepper, chopped finely

1 medium green bell pepper,
   chopped finely

3 cups (1 pound) shredded rotisserie
   chicken

8 large flour tortillas

2 cups coarsely grated cheddar

Guacamole

1 ½ tablespoons finely chopped
   fresh cilantro

1 large tomato, seeded, chopped finely

½ small red onion, chopped finely

2 large avocados (about 1 ¼ pounds),
   chopped coarsely

3 tablespoons fresh lime juice

1 Heat oil in large skillet; cook garlic and onion, stirring, until onion softens. Add spices and bell peppers; cook, stirring, until bell peppers soften. Remove from heat; stir in chicken.

2 Place one tortilla on board; top with ¼ cup of the cheese, then a quarter of the chicken mixture and finally another ¼ cup of the cheese. Top with a second tortilla. Repeat with remaining tortillas, cheese and chicken mixture.

3 Cook quesadillas, one at a time, uncovered, in same large lightly oiled skillet, over medium heat, until golden brown. Turn quesadilla, browned-side up, onto large plate then carefully slide back into skillet, uncooked-side down. Remove from skillet when golden brown on both sides; cover to keep warm while cooking remaining quesadillas.

4 Make guacamole.

5 Serve quesadillas, cut into quarters, with guacamole and sour cream, if desired.

Guacamole Place ingredients in medium bowl; mash with fork to combine.

NUTRITIONAL INFO PER SERVING 66g total fat (23g saturated fat); 54g carbohydrate; 57g protein; 7g fiber; 1051 calories

tomato tarte tatins with crème fraîche sauce

preparation time 40 minutes **cooking time** 30 minutes **serves** 6

9 small firm tomatoes (about 1 ¾ pounds),
   peeled, quartered
2 tablespoons butter
1 clove garlic, crushed
1 ½ tablespoons brown sugar
3 tablespoons balsamic vinegar
¾ sheet frozen puff pastry, thawed
1 egg, beaten lightly
vegetable oil, for deep-frying
6 sprigs fresh basil

Crème fraîche sauce
1 ½ tablespoons butter
2 shallots, chopped finely
1 cup crème fraîche
⅓ cup water

1 Preheat oven to 400°F.

2 Discard pulp and seeds from tomato quarters; gently flatten flesh. Melt butter in large skillet; cook garlic, stirring, over low heat, until fragrant. Add sugar and vinegar; cook, stirring, until sugar dissolves. Place tomatoes in skillet, in single layer; cook, covered, turning once, about 5 minutes or until tomatoes soften.

3 Grease 1-cup metal pie dishes; cut six 4 ½-inch rounds from pastry sheet. Divide tomatoes among dishes, arranging tomoto slices in spiral pattern. Top each with one pastry round, pressing down gently. Brush pastry with egg; bake, uncovered, about 15 minutes or until pastry is browned lightly and puffed.

4 Heat oil in small pot; using metal tongs, place thoroughly dry basil sprigs, one at a time, in pot. Deep-fry about 3 seconds or until basil is crisp. Drain on paper towels.

5 Make crème fraîche sauce.

6 Divide sauce among serving plates; turn tarts onto sauce, top with basil.

Crème fraîche sauce Melt butter in small pot; cook shallots, stirring, about 3 minutes or until softened. Add crème fraîche; cook, stirring, over low heat, until heated through. Stir in the water.

Tip If you cannot find crème fraîche, try substituting sour cream.

NUTRITIONAL INFO PER SERVING 34g total fat (20g saturated fat); 21g carbohydrate; 6g protein; 3g fiber; 415 calories

goat cheese soufflé with creamed spinach sauce

preparation time 15 minutes **cooking time** 25 minutes (plus cooling time) **serves** 6

cooking-oil spray

¼ cup dried breadcrumbs

2 tablespoons butter

3 tablespoons all-purpose flour

1 cup milk

4 eggs, separated

¼ teaspoon cayenne pepper

5 ounces goat cheese, crumbled

Creamed spinach sauce

6 cups baby spinach

⅔ cup heavy cream, warmed

1 Preheat oven to 400°F. Spray six 1-cup soufflé dishes with cooking-oil spray, sprinkle with breadcrumbs turning to coat base and sides of dishes; place on baking sheet.

2 Melt butter in small pot, add flour; cook, stirring, until mixture bubbles and thickens. Gradually add milk; stir until mixture boils and thickens. Transfer to large bowl; stir in egg yolks, pepper and cheese; cool 5 minutes.

3 Beat egg whites in small bowl with electric mixer until soft peaks form; gently fold whites, in two batches, into cheese mixture.

4 Divide mixture among dishes. Bake, uncovered, about 15 minutes or until soufflés are puffed and browned lightly.

5 Make creamed spinach sauce.

6 Serve soufflés with sauce.

Creamed spinach sauce Boil, steam or microwave spinach until just wilted; drain. Squeeze out excess liquid. Blend or process spinach until almost smooth. With motor operating, gradually add cream; process until smooth. Season with salt and pepper to taste.

NUTRITIONAL INFO PER SERVING 26g total fat (15g saturated fat); 9g carbohydrate; 11g protein; 1g fiber; 314 calories

feta and leek triangles

preparation time 15 minutes **cooking time** 15 minutes **serves** 4

7 tablespoons butter

2 cloves garlic, crushed

2 medium leeks (about 1 ½ pounds),
   sliced thinly

1 ½ tablespoons caraway seeds

5 ounces feta cheese, crumbled

⅓ cup coarsely grated cheddar cheese

4 sheets phyllo dough, thawed

2 teaspoons sesame seeds

1 Heat half of the butter in large skillet; cook garlic and leeks, stirring occasionally, until leeks soften. Stir in caraway seeds; cook, stirring, 2 minutes.

2 Combine leek mixture in medium bowl with feta and cheddar.

3 Preheat oven to 400°F. Lightly grease baking sheet.

4 Melt remaining butter in small pot. Brush one sheet of the phyllo lightly with butter; fold in half lengthwise. Place ¼ of the leek mixture at bottom of one narrow edge of phyllo, leaving a ½-inch border. Fold opposite corner of phyllo diagonally across the filling to form a triangle; continue folding to end of phyllo, retaining triangular shape. Place on tray, seam-side down; repeat with remaining ingredients to make four triangles in total.

5 Brush triangles with butter; sprinkle with sesame seeds. Bake, uncovered, about 10 minutes or until browned lightly.

NUTRITIONAL INFO PER SERVING 34g total fat (22g saturated fat); 15g carbohydrate; 14g protein; 4g fiber; 424 calories

asparagus prosciutto frittata

preparation time 25 minutes **cooking time** 20 minutes **makes** 48

6 ounces asparagus (choose thin spears)

6 eggs, beaten lightly

½ cup heavy cream

¼ cup coarsely grated parmesan cheese

3 slices prosciutto (1 ½ ounces)

½ cup drained sun-dried tomatoes,
   chopped finely

1 Preheat oven to 400°F.

2 Boil, steam or microwave asparagus until just tender; drain. Rinse under cold water; drain.

3 Oil an 8- x 12-inch baking pan; line bottom and sides with parchment paper.

4 Whisk eggs, cream and cheese in medium bowl until combined.

5 Place asparagus in pan, in single layer, alternating tips and bases; pour egg mixture over asparagus. Bake, uncovered, about 20 minutes or until firm. Let stand 10 minutes in pan.

6 Cut each slice of prosciutto into 16 squares. Cook prosciutto in medium non-stick skillet, stirring occasionally, until crisp.

7 Cut frittata into 48 pieces; top each with one piece of the prosciutto and ½ teaspoon of the tomato.

Tip The frittata can be made a day ahead and kept covered in the refrigerator.

NUTRITIONAL INFO PER SQUARE 2g total fat (1g saturated fat); 1g carbohydrate; 2g protein; 1g fiber; 27 calories

chicken and olive empanadas

preparation time 25 minutes **cooking time** 40 minutes **makes** 24

2 cups chicken stock

1 bay leaf

3 boneless, skinless chicken thighs

1 ½ tablespoons olive oil

1 small onion, chopped finely

2 cloves garlic, crushed

2 teaspoons ground cumin

½ cup golden raisins

⅓ cup pitted green olives,
   chopped coarsely

5 sheets ready-made piecrust dough

1 egg, beaten lightly

1 Place stock and bay leaf in medium skillet; bring to a boil. Add chicken, reduce heat; poach chicken, covered, about 10 minutes or until cooked through. Cool chicken in liquid 10 minutes; shred chicken finely. Reserve 1 cup of the poaching liquid; discard remainder (or keep for another use).

2 Heat oil in large skillet; cook onion, stirring, until softened. Add garlic and cumin; cook, stirring, until fragrant. Add golden raisins and reserved poaching liquid; bring to a boil. Reduce heat; simmer, uncovered, about 15 minutes or until liquid is almost evaporated. Stir in chicken and olives.

3 Preheat oven to 400°F. Grease two baking sheets.

4 Using 3 ½-inch cutter, cut 24 rounds from sheets of dough. Place 1 heaping tablespoon of the filling in center of each round; fold round in half to enclose filling, pinching edges to seal. Using tines of fork, press around edges of empanadas to make pattern. Place empanadas on baking sheets; brush tops with beaten egg.

5 Bake empanadas, uncovered, about 25 minutes or until browned lightly. Serve with yogurt, if desired.

NUTRITIONAL INFO PER EMPANADA 11g total fat (5g saturated fat); 17g carbohydrate; 5g protein; 1g fiber; 190 calories

pork dumplings

preparation time 25 minutes **cooking time** 15 minutes **makes** 40

8 ounces ground pork
½ cup finely chopped Chinese cabbage
2 green onions, chopped finely
3 tablespoons finely chopped fresh chives
¾-inch piece fresh ginger, grated
2 teaspoons soy sauce
2 teaspoons cornstarch
40 wonton wrappers

Dipping sauce
¼ cup soy sauce
2 teaspoons white vinegar
2 teaspoons brown sugar

1 Combine pork, cabbage, onions, chives, ginger, sauce and cornstarch by hand in medium bowl.
2 Place 1 level teaspoon of the pork mixture into center of each wonton wrapper; brush edges with a little water, pinch edges together to seal.
3 Place dumplings, in batches, in large bamboo steamer. Set over large pot of boiling water; cover, steam about 4 minutes or until cooked through. Remove with slotted spoon; drain well.
4 Make dipping sauce.
5 Serve dumplings with dipping sauce.
Dipping sauce Combine ingredients in small bowl.

NUTRITIONAL INFO PER DUMPLING 1g total fat (0g saturated fat); 4g carbohydrate; 2g protein; 0g fiber; 27 calories

pork satay

preparation time 20 minutes **cooking time** 20 minutes **serves** 4

Soak eight 8-inch bamboo skewers in cold water for at least one hour before use to prevent scorching and splintering.

¾ cup creamy peanut butter

⅓ cup coconut milk

¼ cup sweet Thai chili sauce

⅓ cup chicken stock

1 ½ tablespoons fresh lime juice

1 pound pork tenderloin, sliced into thin strips

2 cups white long-grain rice

3 cups boiling water

¼ cup coarsely chopped roasted unsalted peanuts

⅓ cup coarsely chopped fresh cilantro

1 Preheat oven to 350°F.

2 Combine peanut butter, coconut milk, chili sauce, stock and lime juice in small bowl.

3 Thread pork strips onto eight 8-inch skewers; place, in single layer, in large shallow baking dish; spoon peanut sauce over pork. Bake, uncovered, about 20 minutes or until pork is cooked.

4 Place rice in medium pot with a boiling water, stir until water returns to a boil; cover with tightly fitting lid. Cook rice over low heat for 15 minutes without removing the lid. Remove from heat, still covered, let stand for 5 minutes.

5 Divide rice among serving plates; top with satay sticks and top with peanut sauce, peanuts, and cilantro.

NUTRITIONAL INFO PER SERVING 46g total fat (12g saturated fat); 88g carbohydrate; 50g protein; 8g fiber; 983 calories

chicken skewers with sesame dipping sauce

preparation time 20 minutes **cooking time** 10 minutes **serves** 4

Soak 12 bamboo skewers in cold water for at least one hour before use to prevent scorching and splintering.

12 chicken tenders (2 pounds)

Sesame dipping sauce
¼ cup light soy sauce
3 tablespoons mirin (rice wine)
3 teaspoons white sugar
½ teaspoon sesame oil
1 teaspoon sesame seeds

1 Make sesame dipping sauce.

2 Thread each chicken tenders onto a skewer; brush skewers with half the dipping sauce. Cook skewers, in batches, on heated oiled grill pan until chicken is cooked. Serve skewers with remaining sesame dipping sauce.

Sesame dipping sauce Stir ingredients in small pot over medium heat until sugar dissolves.

Tip Mirin is a sweet rice wine used in many Asian recipes. If it is not available, you can substitute sweet sherry or dry sherry with a pinch of sugar added to it.

NUTRITIONAL INFO PER SERVING 20g total fat (6g saturated fat); 4g carbohydrate; 47g protein; 1g fiber; 393 calories

chipotle beef nachos

preparation time 15 minutes (plus standing time) **cooking time** 40 minutes **makes** 36

2 chipotle chilies

½ cup boiling water

twelve 6-inch corn tortillas

vegetable oil, for deep-frying

1 ½ tablespoons vegetable oil

1 small onion, sliced thinly

1 clove garlic, crushed

10 ½ ounces ground beef

1 ½ tablespoons tomato paste

1 cup beer

¼ cup coarsely chopped fresh cilantro

½ cup sour cream

1 Cover chilies with a boiling water in small heatproof bowl; let stand 20 minutes.

2 Cut three 3-inch rounds from each tortilla. Heat oil in wok or skillet; deep-fry rounds, in batches, until browned lightly. Drain tortilla chips on paper towels.

3 Drain chilies over small bowl; reserve liquid. Remove stems from chilies; discard stems. Blend or process chilies and reserved liquid until smooth.

4 Heat 1 ½ tablespoons of vegetable oil in medium skillet; cook onion, stirring, until softened. Add garlic and beef; cook, stirring, until beef is changed in color. Stir in tomato paste, beer and chili puree; bring to a boil. Reduce heat; simmer, uncovered, about 15 minutes or until liquid is almost evaporated. Stir in cilantro.

5 Top each tortilla chip with rounded teaspoon of the chipotle beef and with ½ teaspoon of sour cream.

NUTRITIONAL INFO PER NACHO 3g total fat (1g saturated fat); 4g carbohydrate; 2g protein; 1g fiber; 57 calories

Pasta & Rice

Many of these pasta and rice dishes will be familiar, some will be familiar with a twist, and some you won't have thought of before. All of them, however, are bound to become favorites.

penne with red pepper and pine nuts

preparation time 15 minutes **cooking time** 20 minutes **serves** 4

2 large red bell peppers (about 1 ½ pounds)

12 ounces dried penne pasta

3 tablespoons olive oil

2 cloves garlic, crushed

½ cup toasted pine nuts

2 fresh small red serrano or jalapeño
   peppers, chopped finely (optional)

¼ cup fresh lemon juice

3 ½ cups baby arugula

3 ½ ounces feta cheese, crumbled

1 Quarter bell peppers; discard seeds and membranes. Roast under broiler, skin-side up, until skin blisters and blackens. Cover pepper pieces in plastic wrap or aluminum foil for 5 minutes, peel away skin then slice thinly.

2 Cook pasta in large pot of boiling salted water, uncovered, until just tender; drain.

3 Heat oil in large skillet; cook garlic, nuts and hot peppers, if using. Cook for 2 minutes or until fragrant. Add bell peppers and lemon juice; stir until hot.

4 Toss pasta and bell pepper mixture in large bowl with arugula and cheese.

Tip You can roast and peel peppers ahead of time and refrigerated until ready to use.

NUTRITIONAL INFO PER SERVING 31g total fat (6g saturated fat); 74g carbohydrate; 21g protein; 8g fiber; 659 calories

risotto with chicken, peas and crispy prosciutto

preparation time 20 minutes **cooking time** 45 minutes **serves** 4

3 cups chicken stock

3 cups water

¾ tablespoon butter

3 tablespoons olive oil

1 small onion, chopped finely

2 cups arborio rice

½ cup dry white wine

12 ounces boneless, skinless chicken
   breasts, chopped coarsely

2 cloves garlic, crushed

1 ½ cups frozen peas

6 slices prosciutto

3 tablespoons finely shredded fresh sage

1 Place stock and the water in pot; bring to a boil. Reduce heat; simmer, covered.

2 Heat butter and half of the oil in large pot; cook onion, stirring, until soft. Add rice; stir rice. Add wine; cook, stirring, until liquid is almost evaporated.

3 Stir in 1 cup simmering stock mixture; cook, stirring, over low heat until liquid is absorbed. Continue adding stock mixture, one cup at a time, stirring, until absorbed after each addition. Total cooking time should be about 35 minutes or until rice is tender.

4 In another skillet, heat remaining oil; cook chicken, stirring, until cooked through. Add garlic; stir until fragrant. Stir chicken mixture and peas into risotto.

5 Cook prosciutto in same skillet until crisp; drain on paper towels then break into chunks. Stir sage and half of the prosciutto into risotto; sprinkle remaining prosciutto over individual risotto servings.

Tip The type of rice you use is the secret of a good risotto. If possible, get one of the traditional risotto rices: arborio, carnaroli or vialone nano. These short, almost opalescent grains release huge amounts of starch during cooking, causing them to absorb the large amount of liquid required to give the risotto its creamy consistency.

NUTRITIONAL INFO PER SERVING 19g total fat (5g saturated fat); 84g carbohydrate; 25g protein; 4g fiber; 666 calories

ravioli with butternut squash and sage sauce

preparation time 15 minutes **cooking time** 25 minutes **serves** 4

1 ½ tablespoons olive oil

8 large fresh sage leaves

1 pound butternut squash,
    cut into ½-inch cubes

4 green onions, chopped coarsely

1 ½ tablespoons thinly shredded
    fresh sage

1 ¾ pounds fresh ravioli or other
    filled pasta

1 ½ tablespoons balsamic vinegar

¾ cup heavy cream

¾ cup vegetable or chicken stock

1 Heat oil in large non-stick skillet; cook sage leaves, stirring gently, until bright green and crisp. Drain on paper towels.

2 Cook squash in same skillet, uncovered, stirring occasionally, about 15 minutes or until browned lightly and tender. Add onion and shredded sage; cook, stirring, 1 minute. Remove from skillet; cover to keep warm.

3 Cook ravioli in large pot of boiling water, uncovered, until they float to the surface; drain. Cover to keep warm.

4 Place vinegar, cream and stock in same skillet; bring to a boil. Reduce heat; simmer, uncovered, 5 minutes. Return squash mixture to skillet; stir over low heat until sauce is heated through. Serve sauce on ravioli; top with sage leaves.

NUTRITIONAL INFO PER SERVING 34g total fat (18g saturated fat); 35g carbohydrate; 18g protein; 4g fiber; 521 calories

pappardelle with chicken and mushroom cream sauce

preparation time 15 minutes **cooking time** 15 minutes **serves** 4

You'll need to buy a rotisserie chicken weighing approximately 2 pounds for this recipe.

3 tablespoons olive oil

1 clove garlic, crushed

1 small onion, chopped finely

8 ounces cremini mushrooms, sliced thinly

¾ cup heavy cream

2 teaspoons finely chopped fresh rosemary

1 ⅓ tablespoons butter

1 pound pappardelle or fettucine

3 cups (1 pound) coarsely shredded cooked chicken

½ cup coarsely chopped roasted walnuts

¼ cup coarsely chopped fresh flat-leaf parsley

¾ cup finely grated parmesan cheese

1 Heat oil in large skillet; cook garlic and onion, stirring, until onion softens. Add mushrooms; cook, stirring, until just tender.

2 Add cream and rosemary to skillet; bring to a boil. Reduce heat; simmer, uncovered, until sauce thickens slightly. Add butter; stir until butter melts.

3 Cook pasta in large pot of boiling salted water, uncovered, until just tender; drain. Return to skillet.

4 Add hot cream sauce, chicken, nuts, parsley and half of the cheese to hot pasta; toss gently to combine. Serve immediately, sprinkled with remaining cheese.

NUTRITIONAL INFO PER SERVING 56g total fat (22g saturated fat); 92g carbohydrate; 55g protein; 9g fiber; 1088 calories

spaghetti with breadcrumbs, garlic and anchovies

preparation time 15 minutes **cooking time** 15 minutes **serves** 4

1 pound spaghetti

12 slices white bread

5 tablespoons butter

2 cloves garlic, crushed

1 ½ ounces drained anchovy fillets,
  chopped finely

2 teaspoons finely grated lemon peel

3 tablespoons fresh lemon juice

½ cup finely chopped fresh chives

½ cup olive oil

1 Cook pasta in large pot of boiling salted water, uncovered, until just tender; drain.

2 Remove and discard crusts from bread; blend or process bread into fine crumbs.

3 Melt butter in medium skillet; cook garlic and crumbs, stirring, until browned.

4 Combine pasta and crumb mixture in large bowl with remaining ingredients; serve with lemon wedges, if desired.

Tip This recipe is best made close to serving.

NUTRITIONAL INFO PER SERVING 45g total fat (13g saturated fat); 126g carbohydrate; 24g protein; 7g fiber; 1019 calories

roasted vegetable lasagna

preparation time 40 minutes (plus standing time) **cooking time** 1 hour **serves** 6

3 medium red bell peppers
  (about 1 ¼ pounds)
2 medium eggplants (about 1 ¼ pounds),
  sliced thinly
3 tablespoons kosher salt
2 medium zucchini, sliced thinly
1 ¼ pounds sweet potatoes, sliced thinly
cooking-oil spray
24-ounce jar pasta sauce
1 package cooked lasagna noodles
5 ounces ricotta, crumbled
1 ½ tablespoons finely grated
  parmesan cheese

White sauce
3 tablespoons butter
¼ cup all-purpose flour
1 ½ cups skim milk
3 tablespoons coarsely grated
  parmesan cheese

1 Preheat oven to 475°F.

2 Quarter bell peppers; discard seeds and membranes. Roast, uncovered, skin-side up, about 5 minutes or until skin blisters and blackens. Cover bell pepper pieces in plastic wrap or aluminum foil for 5 minutes; peel away skin.

3 Reduce oven to 400°F. Place eggplant in colander, sprinkle with salt; let stand 20 minutes. Rinse eggplant under cold water; pat dry with paper towels.

4 Place eggplants, zucchini and sweet potatoes, in single layer, on baking sheets; spray with oil. Roast, uncovered, about 15 minutes or until tender.

5 Make white sauce.

6 Oil deep rectangular 2 ½-quart (10-cup) ovenproof dish. Spread 1 cup pasta sauce over base of dish; top with half of the eggplants and half of the bell peppers. Layer with lasagna noodles; top with ½ cup of the pasta sauce, ricotta, sweet potatoes and zucchini. Top with another layer of noodles, rest of pasta sauce, remaining eggplant and bell peppers. Add another layer of noodles, top with white sauce, sprinkle with parmesan. Bake, uncovered, about 45 minutes or until browned lightly. Let stand 5 minutes before serving with an arugula salad, if desired.

White sauce Melt butter in small pot, add flour; cook, stirring, until mixture thickens and bubbles. Remove from heat, gradually stir in milk; cook, stirring, until sauce boils and thickens. Remove from heat; stir in cheese.

NUTRITIONAL INFO PER SERVING 14g total fat (8g saturated fat); 48g carbohydrate; 15g protein; 8g fiber; 391 calories

baked tortellini and vegetables

preparation time 15 minutes **cooking time** 35 minutes **serves** 4

1 pound tortellini or other filled pasta

1 ½ tablespoons olive oil

7 ounces button mushrooms, sliced thinly

2 medium zucchini, chopped coarsely

1 medium red bell pepper,
   chopped coarsely

26-ounce jar pasta sauce

4 green onions, sliced thinly

¼ cup coarsely chopped fresh
   flat-leaf parsley

2 cups coarsely grated cheddar cheese

1 Preheat oven to 400°F.

2 Cook pasta in large pot of boiling salted water, uncovered, until just tender; drain, reserve ½ cup of the cooking liquid.

3 Heat oil in large skillet; cook mushrooms, zucchini and bell pepper, stirring, until vegetables are just tender. Stir in sauce and reserved cooking liquid; add pasta, onions and parsley, toss to combine.

4 Place tortellini mixture into deep oiled 3-quart (12 cup) ovenproof dish; sprinkle with cheese. Bake, uncovered, about 20 minutes or until lightly browned.

Tip This recipe can be assembled several hours before being reheated and browned in the oven.

NUTRITIONAL INFO PER SERVING 36g total fat (20g saturated fat); 39g carbohydrate; 32g protein; 8g fiber; 620 calories

fresh salmon pasta salad

preparation time 10 minutes **cooking time** 20 minutes **serves** 6

1 pound salmon fillets

1 pound farfalle pasta

1 ½ cups shelled fresh peas

⅔ cup sour cream

1 ½ tablespoons fresh lemon juice

2 teaspoons water

3 tablespoons drained green
    peppercorns, rinsed

1 ½ tablespoons coarsely chopped
    fresh dill

2 celery stalks, sliced thinly on
    the diagonal

⅓ cup coarsely chopped fresh chives

1 Cook salmon, uncovered, in large heated oiled skillet until lightly browned on both sides and cooked to desired degree of doneness. Drain on paper towels.

2 Cook pasta in large pot of boiling salted water, uncovered, adding peas about halfway through cooking time; drain when pasta is just tender.

3 Combine sour cream, lemon juice, water, peppercorns and dill in small bowl.

4 Place salmon in large bowl; using fork, flake salmon. Add celery, chives, sour cream mixture, pasta and peas; toss gently to combine.

Tip Frozen peas can be thawed and substituted for fresh peas; add them to the pasta just before draining it.

NUTRITIONAL INFO PER SERVING 17g total fat (95g saturated fat); 62g carbohydrate; 29g protein; 6g fiber; 536 calories

orzo with fava beans and tomatoes

preparation time 45 minutes **cooking time** 30 minutes **serves** 4

If you cannot find fresh, use 1 pound frozen fava beans.

2 pounds fresh fava beans, shelled

8 ounces orzo pasta

1 ½ tablespoons olive oil

3 green onions, sliced thinly

2 cloves garlic, sliced thinly

1 cup coarsely chopped fresh mint

¼ cup fresh lemon juice

1 pound cherry tomatoes, halved

1 ½ tablespoons brown sugar

1 cup shaved parmesan cheese

1 Boil, steam or microwave beans until just tender; drain. Rinse under cold water; drain. Peel away grey-colored outer shells.

2 Cook orzo in medium pot of boiling salted water, uncovered, until just tender; drain.

3 Heat oil in large skillet; cook onions and garlic, stirring, until onions soften. Add orzo, beans, mint and lemon juice; stir until combined. Transfer to large serving platter.

4 Cook tomatoes and sugar in same skillet, stirring occasionally, about 5 minutes or until tomatoes just soften.

5 Top orzo salad with tomatoes; sprinkle with cheese.

NUTRITIONAL INFO PER SERVING 13g total fat (5g saturated fat); 53g carbohydrate; 28g protein; 16g fiber; 446 calories

eggplant pastitsio

preparation time 40 minutes **cooking time** 1 hour 20 minutes **serves** 8

Pastitsio is to Greeks as lasagna is to Italians – layers of meat and pasta, baked with rich tomato sauce and creamy white sauce.

2 large eggplants (about 2 pounds)
5 ounces linguine or macaroni pasta
2 tablespoons butter, melted
3 eggs, beaten lightly
⅓ cup finely grated parmesan cheese
¼ cup finely chopped fresh basil
¼ cup finely chopped fresh flat-leaf parsley
½ teaspoon ground nutmeg
1 pound ground lamb
1 teaspoon olive oil
1 medium onion, chopped finely
1 clove garlic, crushed
½ teaspoon ground cinnamon
1 ½ tablespoons tomato paste
¼ cup dry red wine
¼ cup beef stock
14 ½-ounce can crushed tomatoes, undrained

White sauce
5 tablespoons butter
⅓ cup all-purpose flour
2 cups milk

1 Preheat oven to 425°F. Cut eggplants lengthwise into very thin slices; place eggplant, in single layer, on oiled baking sheets, cover with aluminum foil. Bake about 25 minutes or until eggplant is softened and browned. Remove from oven.

2 Reduce oven temperature to 350°F.

3 Cook pasta in medium pot of boiling salted water, uncovered, until just tender; drain. Rinse under cold water; drain. Combine in medium bowl with butter, eggs, cheese, herbs and nutmeg.

4 Cook lamb in large, heated non-stick skillet, stirring, until changed in color; remove lamb, drain skillet. Heat oil in same skillet; cook onion and garlic, stirring, about 2 minutes or until onion softens. Return lamb to skillet with cinnamon and tomato paste; cook, stirring, 2 minutes. Add wine, stock and undrained tomatoes; bring to a boil. Reduce heat; simmer, uncovered, stirring occasionally, about 15 minutes or until sauce thickens. (Can be made ahead to this stage. Cover; refrigerate overnight.)

5 Make white sauce.

6 Oil deep 9-inch round cake pan; line bottom and sides with two-thirds of the eggplant. Place half of the pasta mixture in pan; cover with white sauce. Spread lamb sauce over white sauce; top with remaining pasta mixture. Use remaining eggplant to completely cover pastitsio; cover tightly with aluminum foil. Cook about 30 minutes or until heated through. Let stand 10 minutes. Slice into wedges and serve.

White sauce Melt butter in medium pot, add flour; cook, stirring, about 2 minutes or until mixture thickens and bubbles. Gradually stir in milk; cook, stirring, until sauce boils and thickens.

NUTRITIONAL INFO PER SERVING 20g total fat (11g saturated fat); 26g carbohydrate; 24g protein; 5g fiber; 397 calories

creamy chicken, mushroom and asparagus pasta

preparation time 20 minutes **cooking time** 30 minutes **serves** 4

12 ounces rigatoni

5 tablespoons butter

1 ¼ pounds boneless, skinless chicken
    breasts, cut into ½-inch pieces

3 ½ ounces button mushrooms,
    sliced thinly

3 tablespoons all-purpose flour

2 cups milk

½ cup coarsely grated romano cheese

1 ¼ cups coarsely grated cheddar cheese

6 ounces asparagus, trimmed,
    chopped coarsely

¼ cup coarsely chopped fresh
    flat-leaf parsley

1 Preheat oven to 400°F.

2 Cook pasta in large pot of boiling salted water, uncovered, until just tender; drain.

3 Heat a third of the butter in large skillet; cook chicken, in batches,
until browned and cooked through.

4 Heat remaining butter in same skillet; cook mushrooms, stirring, until tender.
Add flour; cook, stirring, 1 minute. Gradually stir in milk. Stir over medium heat
until mixture boils and thickens. Stir in chicken, ¼ cup of the romano, ¾ cup of
the cheddar and the asparagus.

5 Combine chicken mixture and drained pasta in 2 ½ quart (10-cup) ovenproof
dish; sprinkle with remaining cheeses. Bake, uncovered, about 15 minutes or
until top browns lightly. Sprinkle with parsley and serve with a mixed green salad,
if desired.

Tip Rigatoni, a tube-shaped pasta with ridges on the outside, is an ideal pasta
for "pasta al forno" (baked dishes) because it is wide and the hearty fillings cling
to the indentations around the edges.

NUTRITIONAL INFO PER SERVING 37g total fat (22g saturated fat);
75g carbohydrate; 64g protein; 5g fiber; 903 calories

oven-baked risotto with chicken and sun-dried tomatoes

preparation time 10 minutes **cooking time** 35 minutes **serves** 4

1 ½ tablespoons olive oil

1 large onion, sliced thinly

2 cloves garlic, crushed

2 cups arborio rice

¾ cup dry white wine

1 quart (4 cups) chicken stock

4 boneless, skinless chicken breasts
(1 ½ pounds)

3 ½ cups baby arugula leaves

3 ½ ounces sun-dried tomatoes,
sliced thinly

½ cup finely grated parmesan cheese

1 ½ tablespoons coarsely chopped
fresh flat-leaf parsley

1 Preheat oven to 350°F.

2 Heat oil in shallow 3-quart (12 cup) flameproof baking dish or Dutch oven; cook onion and garlic, stirring, until onion softens. Add rice; stir to coat in onion mixture. Stir in wine and stock; bring to a boil. Place chicken, in single layer, on top of rice mixture. Transfer dish to oven; bake, covered, about 25 minutes or until rice is tender and chicken is cooked. Remove chicken; let chicken stand 5 minutes. Slice thickly.

3 Stir arugula, tomatoes and a third of the cheese into risotto; serve risotto topped with chicken. Sprinkle remaining cheese and parsley over chicken.

NUTRITIONAL INFO PER SERVING 21g total fat (6g saturated fat); 93g carbohydrate; 59g protein; 6g fiber; 819 calories

risotto with asparagus and goat cheese

preparation time 10 minutes **cooking time** 30 minutes **serves** 4

3 cups water

3 cups vegetable or chicken stock

1 tablespoon olive oil

2 medium yellow onions, chopped finely

2 cloves garlic, crushed

2 cups arborio rice

½ cup dry white wine

6 ounces asparagus, chopped coarsely

½ cup frozen peas

¼ cup loosely packed fresh thyme leaves

5 ounces goat cheese, crumbled

1 Combine water and stock in medium pot; bring to a boil. Reduce heat; simmer, covered.

2 Heat oil in large pot; cook onions and garlic, stirring until soft. Add rice; stir to coat in onion mixture. Add wine; cook, stirring, until liquid is almost evaporated. Stir in 1 cup simmering stock mixture; cook, stirring, over low heat until stock is absorbed. Continue adding stock, one cup at a time, stirring until stock is absorbed after each addition and rice is tender.

3 Add asparagus, peas, 3 tablespoons of the thyme and 3 ounces of the cheese to risotto; cook, stirring, until asparagus is tender.

4 Serve risotto sprinkled with remaining thyme and cheese.

NUTRITIONAL INFO PER SERVING 12g total fat (5g saturated fat); 90g carbohydrate; 17g protein; 7g fiber; 574 calories

risotto with butternut squash and spinach

preparation time 15 minutes **cooking time** 40 minutes **serves** 4

Chopped fresh pumpkin can be used
in place of butternut squash.

1 pound butternut squash, peeled and
   chopped coarsely
3 tablespoons olive oil
1 ¼ quarts (5 cups) water
1 ½ cups vegetable stock
1 large onion, chopped coarsely
2 cloves garlic, crushed
2 cups arborio rice
½ cup dry white wine
8 cups spinach, chopped coarsely
½ cup toasted pine nuts
½ cup finely grated parmesan cheese
½ cup heavy cream

1 Preheat oven to 425°F.

2 Combine butternut squash and half of the oil in medium baking dish;
roast, uncovered, about 20 minutes or until tender.

3 Combine the water and stock in large pot; bring to a boil. Reduce heat;
simmer, covered.

4 Heat remaining oil in large pot; cook onion and garlic, stirring, until onion
softens. Add rice; stir to coat rice in oil mixture. Add wine; cook, stirring, until
liquid is almost evaporated. Stir in ½ cup simmering stock mixture; cook, stirring,
over low heat until liquid is absorbed. Continue adding stock mixture, one cup
at a time, stirring until absorbed after each addition. Total cooking time should
be about 35 minutes or until rice is just tender.

5 Add spinach, nuts, cheese and cream to risotto; cook, stirring, until spinach
wilts. Add squash; stir gently into risotto.

NUTRITIONAL INFO PER SERVING 41g total fat (14g saturated fat);
91g carbohydrate; 19g protein; 6g fiber; 846 calories

lemon dill risotto cakes

preparation time 20 minutes **cooking time** 1 hour (plus refrigeration time) **serves** 6

3 cups water

2 cups vegetable or chicken stock

1 ½ tablespoons olive oil

1 medium onion, chopped finely

2 cloves garlic, crushed

2 cups arborio rice

1 cup dry white wine

1 ½ tablespoons finely grated lemon peel

3 tablespoons finely chopped fresh dill

2 heads radicchio, chopped coarsely

Lemon dill dressing

1 ½ tablespoons fresh lemon juice

3 tablespoons finely chopped fresh dill

1 ½ tablespoons olive oil

1 ½ tablespoons cider vinegar

1 ½ tablespoons Dijon mustard

1 Combine the water and stock in pot; bring to a boil. Reduce heat; simmer, covered.

2 Heat oil in large pot; cook onion and garlic, stirring, until soft. Add rice; stir to coat rice in onion mixture. Add wine; cook, stirring, until liquid is absorbed. Add ½ cup of the simmering stock; cook, stirring, over low heat until stock is absorbed. Continue adding stock, ½ cup at a time, stirring, until stock is absorbed after each addition. Total cooking time should be about 35 minutes or until rice is tender. Stir in lemon peel and dill. Cool risotto 10 minutes. Cover; refrigerate 2 hours.

3 Make lemon dill dressing.

4 Shape risotto into 18 risotto cakes. Heat large lightly oiled skillet; cook cakes, in batches, until browned lightly on both sides. Cover to keep warm.

5 Cook radicchio, stirring, in same skillet until just wilted.

6 Serve risotto cakes with radicchio, drizzled with dressing.

Lemon dill dressing Combine ingredients in small bowl.

NUTRITIONAL INFO PER SERVING 7g total fat (1g saturated fat); 55g carbohydrate; 6g protein; 4g fiber; 340 calories

chicken jambalaya

preparation time 15 minutes **cooking time** 30 minutes **serves** 4

One of the most well-known Creole dishes, jambalaya is believed to have been devised when a New Orleans cook named Jean tossed together — or "balayez" in the dialect of Louisiana — various leftovers and came up with such a delicious dish that diners named it "Jean Balayez."

1 ½ tablespoons olive oil

1 medium onion, chopped coarsely

1 medium red bell pepper,
  chopped coarsely

1 clove garlic, crushed

2 celery stalks, sliced thinly

1-2 small jalapeño peppers, seeded,
  sliced thinly (optional)

1 ½ cups basmati and wild rice blend

½ cup dry white wine

2 ½ cups chicken stock

14 ½-ounce can crushed tomatoes,
  undrained

1 ½ tablespoons tomato paste

1 ½ pounds chicken andouille sausages

⅓ cup coarsely chopped fresh cilantro

1 Heat oil in large pot; cook onion, bell pepper, garlic, celery and jalapeños, stirring, until vegetables soften. Stir in rice, wine, stock, undrained tomatoes and tomato paste; bring to a boil. Reduce heat; simmer, covered, about 20 minutes or until liquid is absorbed.

2 Cook sausages in large skillet until browned and cooked through. Drain on paper towels; slice thickly.

3 Stir sausages and cilantro into jambalaya mixture just before serving.

NUTRITIONAL INFO PER SERVING 46g total fat (14g saturated fat); 72g carbohydrate; 30g protein; 9g fiber; 853 calories

balti biryani

preparation time 20 minutes (plus marinating time) **cooking time** 1 hour 30 minutes **serves** 4

This delectable Indian recipe combines rice and meat with a heady mixture of aromatic spices. Biryanis are traditionally saved for special occasions, but this version is simple enough to prepare any time. Look for balti curry paste at Asian or Middle Eastern markets if your supermarket doesn't carry it.

1 ¾ pounds beef skirt steak,
   cut into ¾-inch cubes
¾ cup balti curry paste
2 cups basmati rice
8 cloves garlic, unpeeled
1 ½ tablespoons ghee or canola oil
4 cardamom pods, bruised
4 cloves
1 cinnamon stick
3 green onions, sliced thinly
2 cups beef stock
¾ cup toasted slivered almonds
¼ cup loosely packed fresh cilantro
2 fresh small red serrano or Thai chilies,
   sliced thinly

1 Preheat oven to 350°F.

2 Combine steak and curry paste in medium bowl, cover; refrigerate 1 hour. Meanwhile, place rice in medium bowl, cover with water; let stand 30 minutes. Drain rice in strainer; rinse under cold water, drain.

3 Place garlic in small baking dish; roast, uncovered, about 20 minutes or until softened.

4 Melt ghee or heat oil in large pot; cook cardamom, cloves, cinnamon and onions, stirring, until fragrant. Add steak mixture, reduce heat; simmer, covered, stirring occasionally, about 45 minutes or until steak is tender.

5 Add rice with stock to pot; simmer, covered, stirring occasionally, about 15 minutes or until rice is just tender.

6 Peel garlic; chop finely. Add garlic, almonds and cilantro to biryani, cover; let stand 5 minutes. Sprinkle biryani with chilies; serve with raita (for recipe see page 121) and Indian flatbread (naan), if desired.

NUTRITIONAL INFO PER SERVING 42g total fat (8g saturated fat); 86g carbohydrate; 59g protein; 10g fiber; 978 calories

gnocchi with chicken, mushroom and pesto cream

preparation time 10 minutes **cooking time** 25 minutes **serves** 4

2 pounds boneless, skinless chicken thighs

1 ½ tablespoons olive oil

2 cloves garlic, crushed

2 shallots, chopped finely

3 ½ ounces fresh shiitake mushrooms,
  sliced thickly

½ cup dry white wine

¼ cup sun-dried tomato pesto

1 ½ cups half-and-half

⅓ cup coarsely chopped fresh basil

1 ¼ pounds fresh or frozen gnocchi

1 Cut each chicken thigh into thirds. Heat oil in large skillet; cook chicken, in batches, until cooked through. Cover to keep warm.

2 Add garlic, shallot and mushroom to same skillet; cook, stirring, 2 minutes. Stir in wine; simmer, uncovered, until liquid is almost evaporated. Stir in pesto and cream; bring mixture to a boil. Remove from heat; stir in basil.

3 Cook gnocchi, uncovered, in large pot of boiling salted water until gnocchi are just tender and float to the surface; drain.

4 Divide chicken and gnocchi among serving plates; drizzle with creamy pesto.

NUTRITIONAL INFO PER SERVING 49g total fat (21g saturated fat); 52g carbohydrate; 53g protein; 5g fiber; 880 calories

Fish

The best fish dishes are those that are the most simple. While there's an incredible variety of seafood and cooking methods in this chapter, the one constant is the respect shown to the simple flavors of fresh fish.

grilled snapper with spicy tomato sauce

preparation time 15 minutes **cooking time** 15 minutes **serves** 4

3 tablespoons olive oil

3 cloves garlic, crushed

3 shallots, chopped finely

14 ½-ounce can diced tomatoes,
   undrained

1 ½ tablespoons dry sherry

1 ½ tablespoons soy sauce

1 teaspoon Asian chili paste (sambal oelek)

2 teaspoons white sugar

4 red snapper fillets (1 ¾ pounds)

3 cups baby spinach

2 teaspoons red wine vinegar

1 Heat half of the oil in small skillet; cook garlic and shallots, stirring, about 1 minute or until shallots soften. Stir in tomatoes, sherry, soy sauce, chili paste and sugar; bring to a boil. Reduce heat; simmer, uncovered, about 10 minutes or until liquid has reduced by half.

2 Cook fish, uncovered, in large, heated, lightly oiled skillet about 3–4 minutes per side for every ½ inch of thickness, or desired degree of doneness.

3 Place spinach in medium bowl with combined vinegar and remaining oil; toss gently to combine. Serve fish with spicy sauce and spinach salad.

NUTRITIONAL INFO PER SERVING 13g total fat (3g saturated fat); 6g carbohydrate; 43g protein; 2g fiber; 317 calories

shrimp cakes with citrus mayo

preparation time 30 minutes **cooking time** 30 minutes **serves** 4

¾ cup fresh orange juice

¼ cup fresh lemon juice

1-inch piece fresh ginger,
   coarsely chopped

1 teaspoon black peppercorns

2 tablespoons white vinegar

½ cup dry white wine

½ cup roasted macadamia nuts

1 ½ pounds peeled cooked fresh
   small shrimp

1 egg, beaten lightly

1 tablespoon grated orange peel

4 green onions, chopped finely

1 ½ cups dried breadcrumbs

1 long loaf crusty bread

2 tablespoons vegetable oil

4 egg yolks

1 cup butter, melted

3 ounces watercress

1 Combine orange and lemon juices, ginger, peppercorns, vinegar, and wine in small pot; bring to a boil. Reduce heat; simmer, uncovered, about 8 minutes or until reduced to ½ cup. Remove from heat; strain into small bowl.

2 Blend or process nuts until finely chopped; place in large bowl. Blend or process 1 pound of the shrimp until mixture forms a paste; place in bowl with nuts. Add remaining ½ pound of the shrimp, egg, orange peel, green onions, and 1 cup of the breadcrumbs; using hands, shape mixture into eight cakes. Press remaining ½ cup breadcrumbs evenly onto both sides of cakes; place on baking sheet.

3 Cut bread into four pieces; split each piece in half horizontally. Toast, cut-side up, under broiler until lightly browned; cover to keep warm.

4 Heat oil in large skillet; cook cakes, in batches, until browned on both sides and heated through. Cover to keep warm.

5 Blend or process egg yolks with citrus reduction until combined. With motor running, add butter in thin, steady stream; process until sauce thickens.

6 Place two pieces of toast on each serving plate; top with watercress and two cakes, drizzle with sauce.

NUTRITIONAL INFO PER SERVING 88g total fat (40g saturated fat); 73g carbohydrate; 59g protein; 6g fiber; 1345 calories

spicy sautéed fish with lemon pistachio couscous

preparation time 30 minutes **cooking time** 20 minutes **serves** 4

1 tablespoon all-purpose flour

1 ½ teaspoons ground cumin

1 ½ teaspoons ground coriander

1 teaspoon sweet smoked paprika

¼ teaspoon cayenne pepper

8 fish fillets (about 1 ½ pounds)
  (such as tilapia or red snapper)

1 tablespoon olive oil

Lemon pistachio couscous

1 cup couscous

2 teaspoons grated lemon peel

¼ cup fresh lemon juice

½ cup pistachios

2 teaspoons olive oil

1 clove garlic, crushed

1 small red onion, chopped finely

½ cup coarsely chopped fresh mint

1 Make lemon pistachio couscous.

2 Combine flour and spices in medium bowl; add fish, and rub spice mixture all over fish.

3 Heat 1 tablespoon olive oil in large skillet; cook fish, in batches, until browned both sides and cooked to desired degree of doneness (about 3–4 minutes per side for every ½ inch of thickness).

4 Serve fish with couscous and, if desired, lemon wedges.

Lemon pistachio couscous Combine couscous, ¾ cup boiling water, lemon peel, and lemon juice in medium heatproof bowl. Cover tightly and let stand about 5 minutes or until liquid is absorbed. Fluff with fork. Meanwhile, heat small skillet; toast pistachios until fragrant, remove nuts. Add oil to same skillet; sauté garlic and onion until onion softens. Stir together nuts, onion mixture, mint, and couscous.

NUTRITIONAL INFO PER SERVING 25g total fat (6g saturated fat); 45g carbohydrate; 50g protein; 3g fiber; 615 calories

shrimp with pistachio potato salad

preparation time 15 minutes **cooking time** 15 minutes **serves** 4

2 pounds uncooked large shrimp

2 teaspoons ground cumin

2 teaspoons ground coriander

1 teaspoon hot paprika

1 clove garlic, crushed

1 lime, quartered

Pistachio potato salad

1 ½ pounds tiny new potatoes, halved

1 cup roasted shelled pistachios,
   chopped coarsely

¼ cup fresh lime juice

3 tablespoons olive oil

4 green onions, sliced thinly

1 medium red onion, chopped finely

1 Peel and devein shrimp, leaving tails intact. Combine cumin, coriander, paprika and garlic in medium bowl, add shrimp; toss shrimp to coat in mixture.

2 Make pistachio potato salad.

3 Cook shrimp mixture on heated oiled skillet or grill pan, uncovered, until changed in color. Add lime; cook until heated through.

4 Serve shrimp and lime with pistachio potato salad.

Pistachio potato salad Boil, steam or microwave potatoes until tender; drain. Place potatoes in large bowl with remaining ingredients; toss gently to combine. Season with salt and pepper to taste.

NUTRITIONAL INFO PER SERVING 28g total fat (3g saturated fat); 32g carbohydrate; 39g protein; 8g fiber; 549 calories

shrimp stir-fry

preparation time 25 minutes **cooking time** 10 minutes **serves** 4

Tamarind paste and puree are tangy Indian seasonings that can be found in Middle Eastern or Asian grocery stores.

2 pounds uncooked jumbo shrimp

3 tablespoons peanut oil

4 green onions, sliced thinly lengthwise

4 cloves garlic, sliced thinly

1 teaspoon cornstarch

½ cup vegetable or chicken stock

3 tablespoons oyster sauce

1 ½ tablespoons tamarind puree

1 teaspoon Asian chili paste (sambal oelek)

2 teaspoons sesame oil

1 ½ tablespoons lime juice

1 ½ tablespoons brown sugar

12 ounces baby yellow squash,
    sliced thickly

10 ½ ounces sugar snap peas, trimmed

1 ¾ pounds baby bok choy,
    chopped coarsely

1 Peel and devein shrimp, leaving tails intact.

2 Heat half of the peanut oil in wok or large skillet; stir-fry onions and garlic, separately, until browned lightly. Drain on paper towels.

3 Blend cornstarch and stock in small bowl; stir in oyster sauce, tamarind, chili paste, sesame oil, lime juice and sugar.

4 Heat remaining peanut oil in same pan; stir-fry shrimp, in batches, until changed in color and almost cooked through. Remove from pan; stir-fry squash until just tender. Add cornstarch mixture; stir-fry until sauce boils and thickens slightly. Return shrimp to pan with peas and bok choy; stir-fry until bok choy just wilts and shrimp are cooked through. Serve with steamed jasmine rice, topped with reserved onion and garlic.

NUTRITIONAL INFO PER SERVING 13g total fat (2g saturated fat); 16g carbohydrate; 34g protein; 7g fiber; 333 calories

tuna skewers with sesame soba noodles

preparation time 20 minutes **cooking time** 10 minutes **serves** 4

Searing the tuna quickly will result in fish that is somewhat rare in the middle, browned on the surface and succulent throughout. Soak 8 bamboo skewers in cold water before use to prevent them from splintering or scorching.

3 tablespoons olive oil

3 teaspoons wasabi paste

1 teaspoon ground coriander

1 ¾ pounds tuna steaks,
    cut into ¾-inch pieces

⅓ cup finely chopped fresh cilantro

10 ½ ounces dried soba noodles

2 to 3 medium carrots, cut into matchsticks

4 green onions, sliced thickly

¼ cup firmly packed fresh cilantro

Mirin dressing

¼ cup mirin (rice wine)

3 tablespoons soy sauce

½-inch piece fresh ginger, grated

1 teaspoon sesame oil

1 teaspoon fish sauce

1 teaspoon sugar

1 Combine oil, wasabi and ground coriander in large bowl, add tuna; toss tuna to coat in mixture. Thread tuna onto eight skewers; sprinkle with chopped cilantro.

2 Cook noodles in large pot of boiling water, uncovered, until just tender; drain. Rinse under cold water; drain.

3 Make mirin dressing.

4 Combine noodles with carrots, onions, cilantro and half of the dressing.

5 Cook skewers on heated oiled grill or grill pan, uncovered, until cooked to desired degree of doneness. Serve on noodles, drizzled with remaining dressing.

Mirin dressing Whisk ingredients together in small bowl.

NUTRITIONAL INFO PER SERVING 23g total fat (6g saturated fat); 53g carbohydrate; 60g protein; 4g fiber; 681 calories

mahi-mahi with roasted corn salad

preparation time 30 minutes **cooking time** 25 minutes **serves** 4

8 ears fresh corn, husks removed

1 egg yolk

1 clove garlic, crushed

2 tablespoons fresh lime juice

1 teaspoon dijon mustard

¾ cup olive oil

1 medium red onion, chopped finely

2 fresh small red serrano or jalapeño
   peppers, chopped finely (optional)

⅓ cup coarsely chopped fresh cilantro

4 mahi-mahi steaks (½-pound)

1 Cook corn on grill pan (or grill) until lightly browned and just tender.

2 Meanwhile, blend or process egg yolk, garlic, lime juice, and mustard until smooth. With motor running, gradually add oil in a thin, steady stream; process until mayonnaise thickens slightly.

3 Using sharp knife, remove kernels from cobs. Place kernels in large bowl with onion, peppers, cilantro, and half of the mayonnaise; toss gently to combine.

4 Cook fish on grill pan (or grill) until browned on both sides and cooked to desired degree of doneness (about 3–4 minutes per side for every ½ inch of thickness). Divide corn salad among serving plates; top with fish, and drizzle with remaining mayonnaise.

Tip Swordfish can be used in place of mahi-mahi, if desired.

NUTRITIONAL INFO PER SERVING 51g total fat (8g saturated fat); 63g carbohydrate; 58g protein; 17g fiber; 974 calories

seared tuna with mashed potatoes and salsa verde

preparation time 25 minutes **cooking time** 20 minutes **serves** 4

Tuna tastes best if browned on both sides but still fairly rare in the middle; overcooking will make it dry.

2 pounds potatoes, peeled and halved (fingerling, baby red, or Yukon Gold)

2 tablespoons butter

1 tablespoon extra-virgin olive oil

four 6-ounce tuna steaks

3 ounces baby arugula leaves

Salsa verde

½ cup firmly packed fresh flat-leaf parsley leaves

¼ cup loosely packed fresh mint leaves

⅔ cup extra-virgin olive oil

¼ cup drained capers, rinsed

2 teaspoons Dijon mustard

2 tablespoons fresh lemon juice

8 drained anchovy fillets

1 clove garlic, quartered

1 Boil, steam, or microwave potatoes until tender; drain. Mash potatoes, butter, and oil roughly in large bowl with potato masher. Cover to keep warm.

2 Make salsa verde.

3 Cook fish, in batches, on grill pan (or grill) until browned on both sides and cooked to desired degree of doneness.

4 Divide arugula and mashed potatoes among serving plates; top with fish, and drizzle with salsa verde.

Salsa verde Blend or process ingredients until just combined. Transfer to medium bowl; whisk before pouring over fish.

Tip Fingerling, red, and Yukon Gold potatoes have thin, tender skin, so you don't have to peel them for mashed potatoes.

NUTRITIONAL INFO PER SERVING 58g total fat (14g saturated fat); 35g carbohydrate; 53g protein; 5g fiber; 884 calories

slow-roasted pesto salmon

preparation time 20 minutes **cooking time** 45 minutes **serves** 8

1 cup loosely packed fresh basil

2 cloves garlic, chopped coarsely

3 tablespoons toasted pine nuts

3 tablespoons fresh lemon juice

¼ cup olive oil

3-pound salmon fillet, skin on

3 tablespoons olive oil

2 large red bell peppers,
    chopped coarsely

1 large red onion, chopped coarsely

1 Preheat oven to 325°F.

2 Blend or process basil, garlic, nuts and juice until combined. With motor running, gradually add ¼ cup of olive oil in thin, steady stream until pesto thickens slightly.

3 Place fish, skin-side down, on piece of lightly oiled aluminum foil large enough to completely enclose fish; coat fish with half of the pesto. Gather corners of aluminum foil together above fish; twist to enclose securely. Place fish on baking sheet; roast about 45 minutes or until cooked as desired.

4 Heat 3 tablespoons of olive oil in large skillet; cook bell peppers and onion, stirring, until onion softens.

5 Place fish package on serving platter, unwrap; top with onion mixture, drizzle with remaining pesto.

NUTRITIONAL INFO PER SERVING 28g total fat (5g saturated fat); 6g carbohydrate; 40g protein; 2g fiber; 431 calories

curried fish fillets with lentils and raita

preparation time 30 minutes **cooking time** 45 minutes **serves** 4

1 cup brown lentils

1 cup green split peas

1 tablespoon vegetable oil

2 medium yellow onions, chopped finely

2 cloves garlic, crushed

2 bay leaves

2 cinnamon sticks

6 cardamom pods

6 whole cloves

½ teaspoon curry powder

¼ teaspoon ground coriander

1 ½ cups chicken stock

four ½-pound halibut or other firm
   white fish fillets

2 tablespoons mild curry paste

½ cup finely chopped fresh
   flat-leaf parsley

Raita

2 cucumbers, seeded

1 cup Greek-style yogurt

1 tablespoon finely shredded fresh mint

1 Cook lentils and split peas in separate medium pots of boiling water, uncovered, until just tender; drain.

2 Make raita.

3 Heat oil in large skillet; cook onions and garlic, stirring until onions soften. Add bay leaves, cinnamon, cardamom, cloves, curry powder, and coriander; cook, stirring until fragrant. Add stock; cook, stirring, 2 minutes. Remove from heat.

4 Spread fish with curry paste; cook on grill pan (or skillet) until browned on both sides and cooked to desired degree of doneness (about 3–4 minutes per side for every ½ inch of thickness).

5 Place lentils, split peas, and parsley in skillet with spicy onion mixture; stir until heated through. Serve fish on lentil mixture; top with raita.

Raita Grate cucumbers coarsely; drain in fine sieve 10 minutes. Combine drained cucumber with yogurt and mint in small bowl.

NUTRITIONAL INFO PER SERVING 19.7g total fat (5.8g saturated fat); 53.5g carbohydrate; 70.4g protein; 15.4g fiber; 706 calories

swordfish in Thai coconut sauce

preparation time 20 minutes   **cooking time** 25 minutes   **serves** 4

If you can't find kaffir lime leaves, you can use 3 teaspoons grated lemon peel instead. Lemongrass can be found in Asian markets; be sure to buy it fresh, not dried.

1 ½ cups jasmine rice

3 ¼ cups coconut milk

4 kaffir lime leaves, sliced

2 fresh small red serrano or Thai chilies, sliced thinly

1 ½-inch piece fresh ginger, chopped finely

1 tablespoon fish sauce

2 tablespoons fresh lime juice

1 tablespoon finely chopped cilantro root or stems

1 tablespoon finely chopped fresh lemongrass

1 tablespoon grated palm sugar or brown sugar

two 1-pound swordfish fillets, skinned

⅓ cup firmly packed cilantro leaves

1   Cook rice in large pot of boiling water, uncovered, until just tender; drain.

2   Combine coconut milk, lime leaves, chilies, ginger, fish sauce, lime juice, cilantro root or stems, lemongrass, and sugar in large skillet; bring to a boil. Reduce heat; simmer, uncovered, 10 minutes. Add fish; simmer, covered, about 10 minutes or until fish is cooked through. Remove from heat; stir in cilantro.

3   Serve fish with coconut sauce on rice.

Tip   Any other firm white fish fillet can be used in this recipe; cooking times will vary depending on the fish used.

NUTRITIONAL INFO PER SERVING   46g total fat (38g saturated fat); 71g carbohydrate; 50g protein; 4g fiber; 908 calories

grilled swordfish with roasted vegetables

preparation time 20 minutes **cooking time** 25 minutes **serves** 4

1 medium red bell pepper,
   cut into thick pieces
1 medium yellow bell pepper,
   cut into thick pieces
1 medium eggplant, cut into thick pieces
2 large zucchini, cut into thick pieces
½ cup olive oil
1 pint cherry tomatoes
¼ cup balsamic vinegar
1 clove garlic, crushed
2 teaspoons sugar
four ½-pound swordfish steaks
¼ cup coarsely chopped fresh basil

1 Preheat oven to 450°F.

2 Combine bell peppers, eggplant, and zucchini with 2 tablespoons of the oil in large baking dish; roast, uncovered, 15 minutes. Add tomatoes; roast, uncovered, about 5 minutes or until vegetables are just tender.

3 Combine remaining 6 tablespoons of the oil, vinegar, garlic, and sugar in screw-top jar; shake well. Brush one-third of the dressing over fish; cook fish, in batches, on grill pan (or grill) until browned on both sides and cooked to desired degree of doneness.

4 Combine vegetables in large bowl with basil and remaining dressing; toss gently to combine. Divide vegetables among serving plates; top with fish.

NUTRITIONAL INFO PER SERVING 34g total fat (6g saturated fat); 9g carbohydrate; 48g protein; 5g fiber; 543 calories

sea bass with white bean puree and herb pesto

preparation time 30 minutes **cooking time** 25 minutes **serves** 4

1 ½ tablespoons olive oil

1 clove garlic, crushed

1 medium onion, chopped finely

three 14 ½-ounce cans white beans,
   rinsed, drained

1 cup chicken stock

¼ cup heavy cream

4 sea bass or red snapper fillets
   (1 ¾ pounds), skin-on

Herb pesto

½ cup finely chopped fresh flat-leaf parsley

¼ cup finely chopped fresh mint

¼ cup finely chopped fresh dill

¼ cup finely chopped fresh chives

1 ½ tablespoons whole-grain mustard

3 tablespoons fresh lemon juice

3 tablespoons drained baby capers,
   rinsed, chopped finely

1 clove garlic, crushed

¼ cup olive oil

1 Make herb pesto.

2 Heat oil in medium pot; cook garlic and onion, stirring, until onion softens. Add beans and stock; bring to a boil. Reduce heat; simmer, uncovered, until almost all liquid has evaporated. Stir in cream; blend or process bean mixture until smooth.

3 Cook fish, skin-side down, in large heated oiled skillet until cooked to desired degree of doneness (about 3–4 minutes per side for every ½ inch of thickness).

4 Serve fish on white bean puree, topped with herb pesto.

Herb pesto Combine ingredients in small bowl.

NUTRITIONAL INFO PER SERVING 24g total fat (4g saturated fat); 7g carbohydrate; 47g protein; 6g fiber; 428 calories

pan fried trout with cider and brandy sauce

preparation time 25 minutes **cooking time** 30 minutes **serves** 4

2 shallots, chopped finely

⅓ cup brandy

⅓ cup sparkling apple cider

¼ cup water

¼ cup heavy cream

1 stick butter, chopped

¼ cup all-purpose flour

1 teaspoon salt

1 teaspoon ground black pepper

four 5-ounce boneless freshwater
   trout fillets

1 ½ tablespoons olive oil

3 cups baby arugula

1 Combine shallots, brandy, cider and water in pot; bring to a boil. Reduce heat; simmer, uncovered, about 5 minutes or until almost all liquid evaporates.

2 Add cream to pot; simmer, uncovered, 5 minutes. Add butter, a few pieces at a time, whisking to combine between additions. Strain sauce into serving pitcher; discard solids. Cover to keep warm.

3 Combine flour, salt and pepper in large shallow dish. Coat fish in flour mixture; shake off excess.

4 Heat oil in large skillet; cook fish on both sides, until browned lightly and cooked to desired doneness (about 3-4 minutes per side for every ½-inch of thickness). Divide arugula among serving plates; top with fish, drizzle with sauce.

NUTRITIONAL INFO PER SERVING 43g total fat (23g saturated fat); 10g carbohydrate; 31g protein; 1g fiber; 587 calories

salmon with white wine tarragon sauce and grilled asparagus

preparation time 10 minutes **cooking time** 25 minutes **serves** 4

1 ¾ pounds potatoes, sliced thickly
1 pound asparagus, trimmed
4 salmon steaks (1 ¾ pounds)

Tarragon sauce
1 ½ tablespoons butter
1 medium onion, chopped finely
½ cup dry white wine
1 ½ cups heavy cream
3 tablespoons finely chopped
   fresh tarragon

1 Make tarragon sauce.
2 Boil, steam or microwave potatoes until just tender; drain.
3 Cook potatoes, asparagus and fish on heated oiled grill or grill pan, uncovered, until potatoes are browned, asparagus is just tender and fish is cooked to desired doneness. Serve fish with potatoes, asparagus and sauce.

Tarragon sauce Melt butter in small pot; cook onion, stirring, until soft. Add wine; bring to a boil. Reduce heat; simmer, uncovered, until liquid reduces by half. Add heavy cream; simmer, uncovered, about 10 minutes or until sauce thickens slightly. Remove from heat; stir in tarragon.

NUTRITIONAL INFO PER SERVING 53g total fat (28g saturated fat); 27g carbohydrate; 52g protein; 5g fiber; 814 calories

blackened trout with brown butter risotto

preparation time 25 minutes **cooking time** 45 minutes **serves** 4

1 teaspoon sweet paprika

1 tablespoon dried thyme

1 tablespoon dried oregano

1 teaspoon cayenne pepper

2 teaspoons garlic powder

four ½-pound trout fillets, skin-on

Brown butter risotto

2 cups water

2 cups vegetable or chicken stock

⅓ cup butter

1 tablespoon olive oil

1 cup dry white wine

1 medium yellow onion, chopped finely

1 clove garlic, crushed

1 ¼ cups arborio rice

¼ cup finely chopped fresh flat-leaf parsley

¼ cup finely grated parmesan cheese

1 Combine spices, herbs, and garlic powder in medium bowl; press spice mixture into skin-side of fish fillets. Cover fish; refrigerate.

2 Make brown butter risotto.

3 Cook fish in large lightly oiled non-stick skillet, skin-side up, until lightly browned. Turn; cook fish until skin browns and fish is cooked to desired degree of doneness (about 3–4 minutes per side for every ½ inch of thickness).

4 Serve fish, skin-side up, on risotto.

Brown butter risotto Combine 2 cups water and stock in medium pot; bring to a boil. Reduce heat, and simmer, covered. Heat butter and oil in large pot until butter begins to brown. Add wine; cook until liquid reduces by half. Add onion and garlic; cook, stirring until onion softens. Add rice, stirring to coat. Stir in ½ cup of the simmering stock; cook over low heat, stirring until liquid is absorbed. Continue adding stock, ½ cup at a time, stirring until liquid is absorbed between each addition. Total cooking time should be about 35 minutes or until rice is tender. Stir in parsley and cheese.

NUTRITIONAL INFO PER SERVING 32g total fat (15g saturated fat); 53g carbohydrate; 51g protein; 1g fiber; 746 calories

bouillabaisse with aïoli and rouille

preparation time 1 hour 15 minutes **cooking time** 40 minutes **serves** 6

1 ½ pounds uncooked large shrimp

2 uncooked medium blue crabs (1 ½ pounds)
   or ½ pound crab meat

10 small tomatoes (about 2 pounds)

1 ½ tablespoons olive oil

1 clove garlic, crushed

1 large onion, chopped coarsely

1 medium leek, chopped coarsely

1 tiny fennel bulb, chopped coarsely

1 fresh small red serrano or Thai chili,
   seeded, chopped coarsely

1 bay leaf

pinch saffron threads

4-inch piece fresh orange peel

1 ½ quarts (6 cups) water

1 cup dry white wine

1 ¾ pounds firm white fish fillets,
   chopped coarsely

1 pound small black mussels

½ cup coarsely chopped fresh
   flat-leaf parsley

1 long French baguette, sliced

Aïoli

3 cloves garlic, quartered

2 egg yolks

3 tablespoons lemon juice

½ teaspoon Dijon mustard

⅔ cup olive oil

Rouille

1 medium red bell pepper

1 fresh small red serrano or Thai chili,
   seeded, chopped finely

1 clove garlic, quartered

1 cup breadcrumbs (preferably stale)

1 ½ tablespoons lemon juice

¼ cup olive oil

1 Peel and devein shrimp, leaving tails intact. Reserve shells; place shrimp meat in medium bowl. Slide knife under top of crab shell at back, lever off; reserve with shrimp shells. Discard gills; rinse crabs under cold water. Cut crab bodies into quarters; place in bowl with shrimp meat.

2 Chop four of the tomatoes coarsely; reserve with seafood shells.

3 Core then cut shallow crosses in bottoms of remaining tomatoes, place in large heatproof bowl; cover with boiling water. Let stand 2 minutes; drain then peel, from cross end towards top. Quarter tomatoes; scoop out seeds, reserve with seafood shells. Chop tomato flesh finely; reserve.

4 Heat oil in large pot; cook reserved seafood shell mixture with the coarsely chopped tomatoes, garlic, onion, leek, fennel, chili, bay leaf, saffron and peel, stirring, about 10 minutes or until shells change in color and vegetables soften. Add the water and wine, cover; bring to a boil. Reduce heat; simmer, covered, 10 minutes. Remove crab shells.

5 Blend or process seafood mixture, in batches, until smooth; using wooden spoon, push each batch through large sieve into large pot. Discard solids in sieve. Reserve ¼ cup strained seafood mixture for rouille (see below). (Can be made ahead to this stage. Cover; refrigerate overnight.)

6 Make aïoli and rouille.

7 Add finely chopped tomatoes to strained seafood mixture; bring to a boil. Add fish and mussels, return to a boil; cook, covered, 5 minutes. Add reserved shrimp meat and crab pieces; cook, covered, further 5 minutes or until mussels open (discard any that do not). Stir in parsley; serve with toasted bread, aïoli and rouille.

Aïoli Blend or process garlic, yolks, lemon juice and mustard until smooth. With motor running, gradually add oil in steady stream; process until aïoli thickens. (Can be made a day ahead. Cover; refrigerate overnight.)

Rouille Quarter bell pepper; discard seeds and membranes. Roast under preheated broiler or at 475°F, skin-side up, until skin blackens. Cover bell pepper pieces in plastic wrap or aluminum foil for 5 minutes; peel away skin, then chop coarsely. Blend or process bell pepper with chili, garlic, breadcrumbs, lemon juice and reserved ¼ cup strained seafood mixture liquid until smooth. With motor running, gradually add oil in thin, steady stream; process until rouille thickens. (Can be made a day ahead. Cover; refrigerate overnight.)

NUTRITIONAL INFO PER SERVING 43g total fat (6g saturated fat); 43g carbohydrate; 55g protein; 7g fiber; 811 calories

seafood orzo paella

preparation time 30 minutes   **cooking time** 30 minutes   **serves** 4

Paella is made using short-grain white rice but, for an alternative, try orzo, a short rice-shape pasta that adds a smoother texture.

2 tablespoons olive oil

1 small yellow onion, chopped finely

4 cloves garlic, crushed

16 ounces dried orzo pasta

pinch saffron threads

1 cup dry white wine

6 small tomatoes, seeded,
   chopped coarsely

2 tablespoons tomato paste

1 teaspoon grated orange peel

4 sprigs fresh marjoram or oregano

4 cups vegetable or chicken stock, warmed

1 ½ cups frozen peas

12 large fresh shrimp, peeled and
   deveined with tails intact

½ pound small mussels, scrubbed
   and debearded

½-pound piece white fish,
   cut into 1-inch pieces

⅓ pound calamari rings

1 Heat oil in large deep skillet; cook onion and garlic, stirring until onion softens. Add orzo and saffron, stirring to coat. Stir in wine, tomatoes, tomato paste, orange peel, and marjoram; cook, stirring until wine has almost evaporated.

2 Add 1 cup of the stock, stirring until absorbed. Add remaining stock; cook, stirring until orzo is almost tender.

4 Place peas and seafood in pan on top of orzo mixture; do not stir to combine. Cover pan, reduce heat, and simmer about 10 minutes or until seafood has changed color and mussels have opened (discard any that do not).

Tip This recipe can be made in a traditional paella pan if you own one; otherwise a deep skillet or wok with a tight-fitting lid will suffice. Serve the paella straight from the pan at the table.

NUTRITIONAL INFO PER SERVING 15g total fat (3g saturated fat); 95g carbohydrate; 58g protein; 9g fiber; 807 calories

steamed mussels with spicy saffron sauce

preparation time 25 minutes **cooking time** 13 minutes **serves** 6

¾ cup dry white wine

¼ teaspoon saffron threads

1 ½ tablespoons fish sauce

2 teaspoons finely grated lime peel

4 ½ pounds medium black mussels

1 ½ tablespoons peanut oil

2-inch piece fresh ginger, grated coarsely

2 cloves garlic, crushed

3 fresh small red serrano or jalapeño
   peppers, sliced thinly (optional)

½ cup loosely packed fresh cilantro

1 Bring wine to a boil in small pot. Stir in saffron, fish sauce and lime peel; remove from heat. Let stand 10 minutes.

2 Scrub mussels; remove beards.

3 Heat oil in large pot; cook ginger, garlic and peppers, stirring, until fragrant. Add wine mixture and mussels; bring to a boil. Reduce heat; simmer, covered, about 5 minutes or until mussels open (discard any that do not).

4 Spoon mussels and broth into serving bowls; sprinkle with cilantro.

NUTRITIONAL INFO PER SERVING 2g total fat (1g saturated fat); 4g carbohydrate; 8g protein; 1g fiber; 108 calories

Thai fish burgers with sweet and sour salad

preparation time 20 minutes **cooking time** 15 minutes **serves** 4

1 pound cod fillets, chopped coarsely

1 ½ tablespoons fish sauce

1 ½ tablespoons kecap manis

1 clove garlic, quartered

1 fresh small red serrano or jalapeño
  pepper, quartered (optional)

2 ounces green beans, trimmed,
  chopped coarsely

¼ cup shredded coconut

¼ cup finely chopped fresh cilantro

1 large flatbread or 4 thick pitas

⅓ cup sweet Thai chili sauce

Sweet and sour salad

2 cups finely shredded iceberg lettuce

½ cup bean sprouts, chopped coarsely

1 hothouse cucumber, seeded,
  sliced thinly

3 tablespoons lime juice

1 ½ tablespoons fish sauce

1 ½ tablespoons brown sugar

1 Blend or process fillets, fish sauce, kecap manis, garlic and pepper until smooth. Place in large bowl with beans, coconut and cilantro; combine ingredients by hand then shape mixture into four burgers.

2 Cook burgers on heated oiled grill pan or skillet, covered, about 15 minutes or until cooked through.

3 Make sweet and sour salad.

4 Cut bread in half; split halves horizontally. Toast, cut-side up. Divide bread among serving plates; top with salad, burgers and chili sauce.

Sweet and sour salad Place ingredients in medium bowl; toss gently to combine.

Tip To make your own kecap manis, heat equal parts soy sauce and brown sugar, stirring until sugar dissolves.

NUTRITIONAL INFO PER SERVING 2g total fat (1g saturated fat); 8g carbohydrate; 8g protein; 2g fiber; 84 calories

chipotle shrimp with pineapple salsa

preparation time 20 minutes **cooking time** 20 minutes **serves** 4

Chipotle peppers are jalapeños that have been dried and smoked. They have a deep, intensely smoky flavor rather than a searing heat.

2 pounds uncooked medium shrimp

2 medium red onions, cut into wedges

1 small pineapple (about 1 ¾ pounds), chopped coarsely

½ cup firmly packed fresh cilantro

Chipotle paste

3 chipotle peppers

3 tablespoons apple cider vinegar

3 tablespoons water

1 small onion, chopped coarsely

2 cloves garlic, quartered

2 teaspoons ground cumin

1 Make chipotle paste.

2 Peel and devein shrimp, leaving tails intact. Combine shrimp in medium bowl with half of the chipotle paste.

3 Cook onions and pineapple on heated oiled griddle or skillet, uncovered, about 10 minutes or until just tender.

4 Cook shrimp on heated oiled griddle or skillet, uncovered, until changed in color.

5 Combine onions and pineapple in medium bowl with cilantro; serve with shrimp and remaining chipotle paste.

Chipotle paste Soak peppers in vinegar in small bowl for 10 minutes. Blend or process mixture with water, onion, garlic and cumin until smooth. Place chipotle paste in small pot; bring to a boil. Reduce heat; simmer, uncovered, about 10 minutes or until paste thickens.

Tip If you are pressed for time, substitute chipotle paste with chipotles in adobo sauce or pureed chipotles in adobe sauce, which are both available in most supermarkets.

NUTRITIONAL INFO PER SERVING 1g total fat (0g saturated fat); 14g carbohydrate; 28g protein; 4g fiber; 189 calories

Chicken

Probably the most versatile meat, chicken's mild taste lends itself to every type of flavoring. The recipes in this chapter showcase the many ways chicken can be cooked as well as the many cuisines in which it's used.

honey mustard chicken with creamy fennel slaw

preparation time 20 minutes **cooking time** 30 minutes **serves** 4

3 tablespoons honey

2 teaspoons Dijon mustard

4 boneless, skinless chicken breasts
   (1 ½ pounds)

Creamy fennel slaw

2 medium fennel bulbs (about 1 ¼ pounds)

3 celery stalks, sliced thinly

¼ cup coarsely chopped fresh
   flat-leaf parsley

2 teaspoons Dijon mustard

3 tablespoons fresh lemon juice

3 tablespoons light sour cream

2 cloves garlic, crushed

¼ cup low-fat mayonnaise

1 Combine honey and mustard in small bowl. Brush chicken on both sides with half of the honey mixture; cook in batches, in large, heated, lightly oiled skillet about 15 minutes or until cooked through, brushing with remaining honey mixture.

2 Make creamy fennel slaw.

3 Serve chicken with slaw, sprinkled with reserved fennel tips.

Creamy fennel slaw Trim fennel, reserving about 1 ½ tablespoons of the tips (discard the rest). Slice fennel thinly; combine with celery and parsley in large bowl. Place remaining ingredients in small bowl, pour over slaw mixture; toss gently to combine.

NUTRITIONAL INFO PER SERVING 9g total fat (3g saturated fat); 21g carbohydrate; 41g protein; 5g fiber; 328 calories

crispy salt-and-pepper chicken

preparation time 15 minutes **cooking time** 30 minutes **serves** 4

2 teaspoons sea salt

2 teaspoons cracked black peppercorns

1 teaspoon crushed red pepper flakes

four ½-pound chicken breast fillets,
  skin on

12 ounces gai larn, chopped coarsely

1 tablespoon oyster sauce

2 teaspoons sesame oil

¼ cup firmly packed fresh cilantro leaves

2 green onions, sliced thinly lengthwise

1 Combine salt, pepper, crushed red pepper and chicken in large bowl.

2 Cook chicken, skin-side down, in oiled skillet about 10 minutes or until browned and crisp. Turn chicken; cook about 5 minutes or until cooked through. Remove from pan, cover, and keep warm.

3 Stir-fry gai larn, oyster sauce and sesame oil in skillet until gai larn is wilted.

4 Serve chicken with gai larn, sprinkled with cilantro and onions. Serve with lime wedges, if desired.

Tip Gai larn is also called Chinese broccoli. You can substitute broccoli rabe or bok choy.

NUTRITIONAL INFO PER SERVING 16g total fat (4g saturated fat); 3g carbohydrate; 44g protein; 2g fiber; 335 calories

chicken with rosemary and garlic

preparation time 20 minutes **cooking time** 55 minutes **serves** 4

8 chicken thighs (3 pounds), skin on

3 tablespoons all-purpose flour

2 teaspoons sweet paprika

1 teaspoon ground black pepper

1 ½ tablespoons olive oil

4 cloves garlic, unpeeled

2 sprigs fresh rosemary

1 ½ cups chicken stock

½ cup dry white wine

1 Preheat oven to 350°F.

2 Toss chicken in combined flour, paprika and pepper; shake away excess flour mixture from chicken.

3 Heat oil in large ovenproof skillet; cook chicken, in batches, until browned all over.

4 Return chicken to same skillet with garlic, rosemary, stock and wine; bring to a boil. Transfer skillet to oven; cook, uncovered, about 40 minutes or until chicken is tender and cooked through.

5 Remove chicken from skillet; cover to keep warm. Cook pan juices in same skillet over medium heat, uncovered, about 5 minutes or until sauce thickens slightly. Divide chicken among serving plates, drizzle with sauce.

NUTRITIONAL INFO PER SERVING 40g total fat (12g saturated fat); 6g carbohydrate; 43g protein; 1g fiber; 582 calories

honey soy chicken salad

preparation time 20 minutes **cooking time** 15 minutes **serves** 4

1 ¼ pounds boneless, skinless chicken
breasts, sliced thinly

3 tablespoons soy sauce

⅓ cup honey

1 clove garlic, crushed

4 fresh small red serrano or Thai chilies,
seeded, chopped finely (optional)

10 ½ ounces snow peas

2 medium carrots

1 ½ tablespoons peanut oil

2 cups finely shredded savoy cabbage

1 medium yellow bell pepper, sliced thinly

1 medium red bell pepper, sliced thinly

1 cucumber, seeded, sliced thinly

4 green onions, sliced thinly

½ cup loosely packed fresh mint

3 tablespoons fresh lime juice

2 teaspoons sesame oil

1 Place chicken in medium bowl with soy auce, honey, garlic and half of the chilies; toss to coat chicken in chili mixture. Cover; refrigerate until required.

2 Boil, steam or microwave snow peas until just tender; drain. Rinse immediately under cold water; drain. Using vegetable peeler, slice carrots into ribbons.

3 Heat peanut oil in wok or large skillet; stir-fry drained chicken, in batches, until browned and cooked through.

4 Place chicken, snow peas and carrots in large serving bowl with remaining ingredients and remaining chilies; toss gently to combine.

Tip You can use a large rotisserie chicken instead of cooking the chicken yourself. Shred the meat coarsely before tossing with remaining salad ingredients.

NUTRITIONAL INFO PER SERVING 11g total fat (2g saturated fat); 23g carbohydrate; 47g protein; 4g fiber; 381 calories

citrus grilled chicken

preparation time 10 minutes (plus refrigeration time) **cooking time** 20 minutes **serves** 4

⅔ cup fresh lemon juice

¾ cup fresh orange juice

3 cloves garlic, crushed

1 ½ tablespoons finely chopped
   fresh oregano

1 teaspoon ground cumin

1 fresh small red serrano or jalapeño
   pepper, chopped finely

1 ½ tablespoons olive oil

4 boneless, skinless chicken breasts

3 ears fresh corn (about 1 ¾ pounds),
   shucked, quartered

1 large orange, unpeeled, cut into
   eight wedges

8 green onions, cut into 3-inch lengths

1 Combine juices, garlic, oregano, cumin, chili and oil in medium bowl, add chicken; toss chicken to coat in marinade. Cover; refrigerate overnight, if possible.

2 Drain chicken; reserve marinade. Cook chicken on heated oiled grill or grill pan, uncovered, until cooked through.

3 Cook corn, orange and onions on heated oiled grill or grill pan, uncovered, until they are tender.

4 Place reserved marinade in small pot; bring to a boil. Reduce heat; simmer, uncovered, 2 minutes. Serve chicken with corn, orange and onions, drizzled with marinade.

NUTRITIONAL INFO PER SERVING 11g total fat (2g saturated fat); 33g carbohydrate; 53g protein; 8g fiber; 459 calories

chicken, mushroom and fennel pies

preparation time 20 minutes **cooking time** 30 minutes **serves** 4

1 ½ tablespoons olive oil

2 cloves garlic, crushed

1 medium leek, sliced thinly

1 small fennel bulb, sliced thinly

7 ounces button mushrooms, quartered

½ cup dry white wine

4 boneless, skinless chicken breasts
   (1 ¾ pounds), chopped coarsely

1 ½ cups heavy cream

1 ½ tablespoons Dijon mustard

¼ cup coarsely chopped fresh
   flat-leaf parsley

1 sheet puff pastry, thawed,
   cut into quarters

1 egg, beaten lightly

1 ½ tablespoons fennel seeds

1 Preheat oven to 400°F.

2 Heat oil in large pot; cook garlic, leek, fennel and mushrooms, stirring, until vegetables soften.

3 Stir in wine; bring to a boil. Reduce heat; simmer, uncovered, 3 minutes. Add chicken and cream; bring to a boil. Reduce heat; simmer, uncovered, about 10 minutes or until chicken is cooked through and sauce thickens slightly. Stir in mustard and parsley.

4 Place pastry quarters onto baking sheet, brush pastry with egg and sprinkle with seeds; bake about 10 minutes or until golden brown.

5 Divide chicken mixture among small serving bowls, top each with pastry.

NUTRITIONAL INFO PER SERVING 53g total fat (29g saturated fat); 21g carbohydrate; 54g protein; 4g fiber; 799 calories

chicken, olive and lemon tagine

preparation time 30 minutes (plus standing time) **cooking time** 2 hours 30 minutes **serves** 8

A tagine is a Moroccan stew. Preserved lemon rind, a popular condiment in North African cuisine, can be difficult to find in the United States. You can make your own substitute by cutting several slits in a lemon and filling them with salt; wrap the lemon in plastic wrap and refrigerate for at least 24 hours.

3 tablespoons all-purpose flour

2 teaspoons hot paprika

8 chicken drumsticks (2 ½ pounds)

8 chicken thighs (3 pounds)

3 tablespoons butter

2 medium red onions, sliced thickly

3 cloves garlic, crushed

1 teaspoon cumin seeds

½ teaspoon ground turmeric

½ teaspoon ground coriander

¼ teaspoon saffron threads

1 teaspoon crushed red pepper flakes

1 teaspoon ground ginger

3 cups chicken stock

14 ½-ounce can chickpeas,
   rinsed and drained

3 tablespoons finely sliced preserved
   lemon peel

⅓ cup pitted green olives

3 tablespoons finely chopped fresh cilantro

Tunisian-style rice

3 cups white long-grain rice

1 ½ tablespoons butter

1 ½ quarts (6 cups) water

1 Preheat oven to 325°F.

2 Place flour and paprika in paper or plastic bag, add chicken pieces, in batches; shake gently to coat chicken in flour mixture.

3 Melt butter in large ovenproof skillet; cook chicken pieces, in batches, until browned. Cook onions in same skillet, stirring, until softened. Add garlic, cumin, turmeric, ground coriander, saffron, red pepper and ginger; cook, stirring, until fragrant. Return chicken with stock to dish; bring to a boil. Bake, covered, 30 minutes. Add chickpeas; cook tagine, covered, 1 hour. (Can be made ahead to this stage. Cover; refrigerate overnight.)

4 Make Tunisian-style rice.

5 Remove tagine from oven. Stir in lemon, olives and fresh cilantro just before serving; serve with rice.

Tunisian-style rice Wash rice in strainer under cold water until water runs clear; drain. Melt butter in large pot, add rice; stir until rice is coated in butter. Add the water; bring to a boil. Reduce heat; simmer rice, partially covered, about 10 minutes or until steam holes appear on the surface. Cover rice tightly, reduce heat to as low as possible; steam 10 minutes (do not remove lid). Remove from heat; let stand 10 minutes without removing lid. Fluff with fork before serving.

NUTRITIONAL INFO PER SERVING 35g total fat (13g saturated fat); 70g carbohydrate; 45g protein; 3g fiber; 775 calories

chicken stuffed with smoked salmon and goat cheese

preparation time 25 minutes   **cooking time** 1 hour 15 minutes   **serves** 4

4 medium potatoes (about 1 ¾ pounds),
   sliced thinly
¼ cup coarsely chopped fresh
   flat-leaf parsley
2 cloves garlic, crushed
1 ½ tablespoons olive oil
⅔ cup milk, warmed
3 tablespoons finely chopped fresh chives
3 ½ ounces soft goat cheese
4 boneless, skinless chicken breasts
   (1 ¾ pounds)
4 slices smoked salmon (4 ounces)
2 cups baby spinach

Spinach salad
3 ½ cups baby spinach
1 ½ tablespoons olive oil
3 tablespoons fresh lemon juice
1 clove garlic, crushed

1 Preheat oven to 400°F.

2 Combine potatoes, parsley, garlic and oil in medium bowl. Layer potato mixture in 2 ½-quart (10-cup) ceramic baking dish; pour milk over mixture. Roast, uncovered, about 40 minutes or until potatoes are just tender.

3 Combine chives and cheese in small bowl. Cut breasts in half horizontally almost all the way through; open each breast. Spread each fillet with a quarter of the cheese mixture; top with one slice of salmon and a quarter of the spinach. Roll each fillet tightly to enclose filling; secure with toothpicks.

4 Cook chicken in large oiled skillet, uncovered, until browned.

5 Place chicken on cooked potatoes; roast, uncovered, about 15 minutes or until chicken is cooked through. Let stand 5 minutes; remove toothpicks, slice chicken thickly.

6 Make spinach salad.

7 Serve chicken with potatoes and salad.

Spinach salad   Place ingredients in medium bowl: toss gently to combine.

NUTRITIONAL INFO PER SERVING 21g total fat (6g saturated fat);
26g carbohydrate; 62g protein; 4g fiber; 554 calories

chicken stuffed with ricotta, basil and prosciutto

preparation time 30 minutes **cooking time** 2 hours **serves** 4

8 chicken thighs (3 pounds)

⅔ cup ricotta cheese

4 slices prosciutto (2 ounces),
　halved lengthwise

8 large fresh basil leaves

1 ½ tablespoons olive oil

1 medium onion, chopped finely

3 large carrots, chopped finely

1 celery stalk, chopped finely

2 cloves garlic, chopped finely

3 tablespoons tomato paste

½ cup dry white wine

8 small tomatoes (about 1 ½ pounds),
　peeled, chopped coarsely

14 ½-ounce can diced tomatoes,
　undrained

½ cup water

1 Preheat oven to 325°F.

2 Using small sharp knife, cut a pocket through thickest part of each chicken thigh over the bone, push 1 ½ tablespoons of the cheese, one slice of prosciutto and one basil leaf into each pocket; secure pocket closed with toothpick.

3 Heat oil in large deep ovenproof skillet; cook chicken, in batches, until browned all over.

4 Cook onion, carrots, celery and garlic in same skillet, stirring, about 5 minutes or until onion softens. Add tomato paste; cook, stirring, 2 minutes. Add wine; bring to a boil. Reduce heat; simmer, uncovered, 1 minute. Add chopped tomatoes, canned tomatoes and water; bring to a boil. Reduce heat; simmer, uncovered, 10 minutes.

5 Return chicken to skillet, cover; transfer to oven, cook 1 hour. Uncover; cook about 20 minutes or until chicken is cooked through. Remove toothpicks; serve chicken with crusty bread, if desired.

NUTRITIONAL INFO PER SERVING 47g total fat (16g saturated fat); 11g carbohydrate; 53g protein; 6g fiber; 699 calories

lemon chicken with spinach salad

preparation time 15 minutes **cooking time** 15 minutes **serves** 4

12 chicken tenders (2 pounds)
3 tablespoons fresh lemon juice
1 ½ tablespoons fresh thyme
½ cup olive oil
3 ½ cups baby spinach leaves
1 small red onion, chopped finely
8 ounces cherry tomatoes, halved
3 ounces snow pea sprouts
⅓ cup red wine vinegar
½ teaspoon Dijon mustard

1 Place chicken in large bowl with lemon juice, thyme and 3 tablespoons of the oil; toss to coat chicken in lemon mixture. Cook chicken, in batches, on heated oiled skillet or grill pan until browned and cooked through.

2 Combine spinach, onion, tomatoes and sprouts in large bowl. Combine remaining oil, vinegar and mustard in screw-top jar; shake well. Drizzle dressing over salad; toss gently to combine. Serve salad topped with chicken.

NUTRITIONAL INFO PER SERVING 34g total fat (5g saturated fat); 8g carbohydrate; 54g protein; 3g fiber; 557 calories

Moroccan chicken with couscous

preparation time 10 minutes (plus standing time) **cooking time** 10 minutes **serves** 4

Check your Middle Eastern market for preserved lemons, which are salted lemons preserved in a mixture of olive oil and lemon juice. You can make your own substitute by cutting several slits in a lemon and filling them with salt; wrap in plastic and refrigerate for at least 24 hours

4 single boneless, skinless
   chicken breasts (1 ½ pounds)
2 cups vegetable or chicken stock
2 cups couscous
1 ½ tablespoons butter
1 small red onion, sliced thinly
2 fresh small red serrano or Thai chilies,
   seeded, chopped finely
½ cup coarsely chopped pitted prunes
⅓ cup slivered almonds, toasted
½ cup coarsely chopped fresh mint
¼ cup finely chopped preserved
   lemon peel

Moroccan marinade
2 teaspoons ground cumin
1 teaspoon paprika
½ teaspoon ground coriander
1 tablespoon olive oil

1 Make Moroccan marinade.

2 Toss chicken in large bowl with marinade; let stand 10 minutes. Cook chicken, in batches, on heated oiled grill or grill pan until browned lightly and cooked through. Let stand 5 minutes; slice chicken thickly.

3 Bring stock to a boil in medium pot. Remove from heat; stir in couscous and butter. Cover; let stand 5 minutes or until liquid is absorbed. Fluff couscous with fork, stir in remaining ingredients.

4 Serve chicken on couscous.

Moroccan marinade   Combine ingredients in small bowl.

NUTRITIONAL INFO PER SERVING 24g total fat (5g saturated fat); 91g carbohydrate; 64g protein; 8g fiber; 851 calories

Cajun chicken with bacon and pineapple salsa

preparation time 15 minutes   **cooking time** 15 minutes   **serves** 4

1 ½ tablespoons sweet paprika

1 teaspoon cayenne pepper

2 teaspoons garlic powder

2 teaspoons dried oregano

1 ½ tablespoons olive oil

8 boneless, skinless chicken thighs
   (2 pounds)

Bacon and pineapple salsa

7 slices bacon

1 small pineapple (about 1 ¾ pounds),
   chopped finely

1 fresh small red serrano or jalapeño
   pepper, chopped finely

¼ cup coarsely chopped fresh
   flat-leaf parsley

1 medium red bell pepper,
   chopped coarsely

¼ cup fresh lime juice

1 teaspoon olive oil

1 Combine spices, oregano and oil in large bowl, add chicken; toss chicken to coat in mixture.

2 Make bacon and pineapple salsa.

3 Cook chicken on heated oiled grill pan or skillet, uncovered, until cooked through.

4 Serve chicken with salsa and lemon wedges, if desired.

Bacon and pineapple salsa Cook bacon on heated skillet, uncovered, until crisp; drain, chop coarsely. Place bacon in medium bowl with remaining ingredients; toss gently to combine.

NUTRITIONAL INFO PER SERVING 31g total fat (0g saturated fat); 11g carbohydrate; 56g protein; 3g fiber; 550 calories

lemon pepper roast chicken

preparation time 35 minutes **cooking time** 1 hour 50 minutes **serves** 4

2 whole heads of garlic

4 ½-pound chicken

cooking-oil spray

2 teaspoons salt

3 tablespoons cracked black pepper

1 medium lemon, cut into eight wedges

1 cup water

3 medium artichokes (about 1 ¼ pounds)

3 tablespoons fresh lemon juice

2 medium red onions, quartered

3 baby fennel bulbs, trimmed, halved

2 medium leeks (about 1 ½ pounds),
   halved lengthwise then quartered

8 ounces cherry tomatoes

⅓ cup dry white wine

¼ cup fresh lemon juice

1 Preheat oven to 400°F.

2 Separate cloves from each garlic head, leaving skin intact. Wash chicken under cold water; pat dry inside and out with paper towels. Coat chicken with cooking-oil spray; press combined salt and pepper onto skin and inside cavity. Place garlic and lemon inside cavity; tie legs together with kitchen string. Place chicken on small wire rack in large ovenproof baking dish, pour 1 cup of water in baking dish; roast, uncovered, 50 minutes.

3 Discard outer leaves from artichokes; cut tough tips from remaining leaves. Trim and peel stalks. Quarter artichokes lengthwise; using teaspoon remove tough centers. Cover artichokes with cold water in medium bowl, stir in 3 tablespoons of lemon juice; soak artichokes until ready to cook.

4 Add drained artichokes, onions, fennel and leeks to dish with chicken; coat with cooking-oil spray. Roast, uncovered, about 40 minutes or until vegetables are just tender.

5 Add tomatoes to dish; roast, uncovered, about 20 minutes or until tomatoes soften and chicken is cooked through. Place chicken on serving dish and vegetables in large bowl; cover to keep warm.

6 Stir wine and ¼ cup lemon juice with pan juices into a medium skillet; bring to a boil. Boil 2 minutes then strain sauce over vegetables; toss gently to combine.

7 Discard garlic and lemon from cavity; serve chicken with vegetables.

NUTRITIONAL INFO PER SERVING 42g total fat (13g saturated fat); 20g carbohydrate; 60g protein; 15g fiber; 723 calories

Greek chicken with olives and artichokes

preparation time 15 minutes **cooking time** 1 hour **serves** 4

3 tablespoons olive oil

12 chicken drumsticks (4 pounds)

1 medium white onion, chopped finely

3 cloves garlic, crushed

1 ½ tablespoons finely grated lemon peel

1 ½ cups chicken stock

½ cup dry white wine

12-ounce jar marinated artichokes,
   drained, quartered

1 pound dried orzo pasta

3 tablespoons finely chopped
   fresh oregano

1 cup pitted Kalamata olives

1 ½ tablespoons finely grated lemon peel

¼ cup fresh lemon juice

1 Heat half of the oil in large heavy-based pot; cook drumsticks, in batches, until browned all over.

2 Heat remaining oil in same pot; cook onion and garlic, stirring, until onion softens. Add 1 ½ tablespoons of lemon peel, stock, wine and artichokes; bring to a boil. Return drumsticks to pot, reduce heat; simmer, covered, 20 minutes. Uncover; simmer, about 10 minutes or until drumsticks are cooked through.

3 Cook orzo in pot of boiling salted water, uncovered, until just tender; drain.

4 Remove chicken from pot; stir oregano, olives, 1 ½ tablespoons of lemon peel and lemon juice into sauce. Serve chicken with sauce on orzo.

NUTRITIONAL INFO PER SERVING 45g total fat (12g saturated fat); 99g carbohydrate; 68g protein; 6g fiber; 1108 calories

chicken kofta with red pepper walnut sauce

preparation time 20 minutes   **cooking time** 20 minutes   **serves** 4

Soak 12 bamboo skewers in cold water for at least one hour before use to prevent scorching and splintering.

1 ½ pounds ground chicken

1 large onion, chopped finely

1 ½ cups dried breadcrumbs

1 egg

¼ cup finely chopped fresh cilantro

½ teaspoon ground cinnamon

3 teaspoons ground cumin

2 teaspoons ground allspice

6 pita pockets, halved

3 ½ cups baby arugula

Red pepper walnut sauce

2 medium red bell peppers

⅓ cup roasted walnuts

3 tablespoons dried breadcrumbs

3 tablespoons fresh lemon juice

1 teaspoon chili paste

½ teaspoon ground cumin

3 tablespoons olive oil

1 Combine chicken, onion, breadcrumbs, egg, cilantro and spices by hand in large bowl; shape ¼ cups of the mixture around each skewer to form slightly flattened sausage shapes. Place kofta on baking sheet, cover; refrigerate 10 minutes.

2 Make red pepper walnut sauce.

3 Cook kofta on heated oiled grill or grill pan, uncovered, about 15 minutes or until cooked through. Serve kofta with warm pita, arugula and sauce.

Red pepper walnut sauce Quarter bell peppers; discard seeds and membranes. Cook on heated oiled grill or grill pan, skin-side down, uncovered, until skin blisters and blackens. Cover pepper pieces with plastic wrap or aluminum foil for 5 minutes; peel away skin. Blend or process bell pepper with remaining ingredients until smooth.

NUTRITIONAL INFO PER SERVING 28g total fat (4.7g saturated fat); 87.2g carbohydrate; 57g protein; 7.2g fiber; 849 calories

cashew crusted chicken breasts with tomato salad

preparation time 20 minutes **cooking time** 20 minutes **serves** 4

¾ cup roasted unsalted cashews

¾ cup fresh flat-leaf parsley,
  chopped finely

1 cup breadcrumbs (preferably stale)

2 eggs

4 chicken breasts (1 ½ pounds)

⅓ cup all-purpose flour

2 tablespoons olive oil

8 ounces arugula leaves

1 pint yellow grape tomatoes, halved

1 medium red bell pepper, sliced thinly

Mustard vinaigrette

1 ½ tablespoons olive oil

1 clove garlic, crushed

1 tablespoon white vinegar

2 teaspoons whole-grain mustard

1 Preheat oven to 350°F.

2 Process nuts in a blender or food processor until they resemble a coarse meal; combine with parsley and breadcrumbs in medium shallow bowl. Beat eggs lightly in another medium shallow bowl.

3 Halve chicken pieces diagonally; slice through each piece horizontally. Coat pieces in flour; shake off excess. Dip chicken in egg, then in breadcrumb mixture.

4 Heat oil in large skillet; cook chicken, in batches, until browned on both sides. Place chicken on greased baking sheet; bake, uncovered, about 10 minutes or until cooked through.

5 Make mustard vinaigrette.

6 Place arugula, tomatoes, and bell pepper in large bowl with vinaigrette; toss gently to combine. Serve salad with chicken.

Mustard vinaigrette Place ingredients in screw-top jar; shake well.

NUTRITIONAL INFO PER SERVING 45g total fat (9g saturated fat); 30g carbohydrate; 58g protein; 6g fiber; 767 calories

lemongrass-skewered chicken with Thai noodle salad

preparation time 20 minutes (plus refrigeration time) **cooking time** 20 minutes **serves** 4

Lemongrass can be found in Asian markets. Be sure to buy it fresh, not dried.

2 pounds boneless, skinless chicken
    breasts, cut into 1 ¼-inch pieces
six 6-inch-long fresh lemongrass sticks,
    halved lengthwise
3 tablespoons peanut oil
1 ½ tablespoons finely grated lime peel
3 tablespoons finely chopped fresh cilantro
1 fresh small red serrano or Thai chili,
    chopped finely

Thai noodle salad
7 ounces bean thread (cellophane) noodles
4-inch stick fresh lemongrass,
    chopped finely
3 tablespoons fresh lime juice
1 clove garlic, crushed
1 fresh small red serrano or Thai chili,
    chopped finely
3 tablespoons fish sauce
1 ½ tablespoons water
1 ½ tablespoons rice vinegar
4 green onions, chopped coarsely
1 medium red bell pepper, sliced thinly

1 Using tip of small knife, cut slit through center of each piece of chicken; thread chicken onto lemongrass skewers. Combine oil, lemon peel, cilantro and chili in shallow baking dish, add skewers; turn skewers to coat in marinade. Cover; refrigerate overnight, if possible.

2 Make Thai noodle salad.

3 Drain skewers; discard marinade. Cook skewers on heated oiled grill or grill pan, uncovered, until cooked through. Serve chicken skewers with salad.

Thai noodle salad Place noodles in large heatproof bowl, cover with boiling water; let stand until just tender, drain. When cool enough to handle, using kitchen scissors, cut noodles into random lengths; cool 10 minutes. Combine lemongrass, lime juice, garlic, chili, fish sauce, water and vinegar in large bowl; add noodles with onions and bell pepper, toss gently to combine.

Tip You can also use bamboo skewers for this recipe instead of lemongrass. Soak them in cold water before use to prevent them from splintering and scorching.

NUTRITIONAL INFO PER SERVING 24g total fat (6g saturated fat); 35g carbohydrate; 58g protein; 2g fiber; 592 calories

Thai red curry

preparation time 15 minutes **cooking time** 30 minutes **serves** 4

2 cups jasmine rice

3 tablespoons peanut oil

1 ¾ pounds boneless, skinless chicken
   thighs, chopped coarsely

1 large onion, chopped coarsely

3 cloves garlic, crushed

3 tablespoons red curry paste

1 red serrano or jalapeño pepper,
   halved lengthwise, sliced thinly

1 teaspoon ground cumin

3 baby eggplants, sliced thickly

1 ½ tablespoons fish sauce

3 fresh strips lime peel, sliced thinly

5-ounce can coconut milk

¾ cup water

5 ounces green beans, cut into
   2-inch lengths

⅓ cup loosely packed fresh cilantro

1 Cook rice in large pot of boiling water, uncovered, until just tender; drain.

2 Heat half of the oil in wok or skillet; stir-fry chicken, in batches, until browned.

3 Heat remaining oil in same pan; stir-fry onion and garlic until onion softens. Add curry paste, pepper and cumin; stir-fry until fragrant. Add eggplants; stir-fry until browned lightly.

4 Return chicken to pan with fish sauce, lime peel, coconut milk, water and beans; stir-fry about 5 minutes or until chicken is cooked through and sauce is thickened slightly.

5 Serve curry and rice sprinkled with cilantro, add lime wedges, if desired.

NUTRITIONAL INFO PER SERVING 34g total fat (13g saturated fat); 87g carbohydrate; 46g protein; 6g fiber; 851 calories

sweet and spicy chicken legs with baby bok choy

preparation time 10 minutes **cooking time** 35 minutes **serves** 4

3 cloves garlic, crushed

2-inch piece fresh ginger, grated

⅓ cup hoisin sauce

¼ cup light soy sauce

2 tablespoons fresh lime juice

¼ cup Chinese cooking wine
  (or dry white wine)

1 fresh small red serrano or Thai chili,
  chopped finely

12 chicken drumsticks (4 pounds)

1 tablespoon peanut oil

10 ounces baby bok choy, quartered
  lengthways

¼ cup fresh cilantro leaves

1 lime, cut into wedges

1 Preheat oven to 475°F.

2 Combine garlic, ginger, hoisin sauce, soy sauce, lime juice, wine, and chili in large bowl. Add chicken; toss to coat. Drain chicken, reserving chili lime mixture.

3 Heat oil in large ovenproof skillet; cook chicken, uncovered, about 5 minutes or until browned on all sides.

4 Transfer pan to oven; roast chicken, uncovered, 15 minutes. Reduce oven temperature to 425°F; cook, basting frequently with chili lime mixture, about 15 minutes or until chicken is cooked through.

5 Boil, steam, or microwave bok choy until just tender; drain.

6 Divide chicken and bok choy among serving plates; sprinkle with cilantro. Serve with lime wedges with steamed jasmine rice, if desired.

NUTRITIONAL INFO PER SERVING 37g total fat (11g saturated fat); 10g carbohydrate; 53g protein; 4g fiber; 611 calories

baked pesto chicken with garlic potatoes

preparation time 15 minutes **cooking time** 30 minutes **serves** 4

Pick up fresh mozzarella, store-bought pesto, and roasted red peppers at the supermarket for a quick, homemade dinner.

4 large potatoes (1 ¾ pounds)

4 cloves garlic, peeled

1 ½ tablespoons olive oil

4 boneless, skinless chicken breasts
  (1 ½ pounds)

3 tablespoons basil pesto

3 ½ ounces drained roasted
  red bell peppers in oil

5 ounces fresh mozzarella or buffalo
  mozzarella cheese, sliced thinly

1 Preheat oven to 400°F.

2 Cut unpeeled potatoes into ¼-inch slices; toss with garlic and oil in large baking dish. Roast, uncovered, 10 minutes, stirring occasionally.

3 Using sharp knife, score each fillet, taking care not to cut all the way through. Spread chicken with pesto; top with bell pepper and cheese. Place chicken, topping-side up, on oiled wire rack; sit rack over potatoes in baking dish.

4 Bake chicken, uncovered, about 20 minutes or until chicken is cooked through. Serve chicken with potatoes.

NUTRITIONAL INFO PER SERVING 26g total fat (8g saturated fat); 23g carbohydrate; 48g protein; 4g fiber; 522 calories

slow cooked chicken stew

preparation time 25 minutes **cooking time** 1 hour 50 minutes **serves** 4

3 ½ pounds chicken (assorted pieces
  on the bone)
1 ½ tablespoons olive oil
12 shallots, halved
1 pound baby carrots, trimmed
3 small parsnips, chopped coarsely
1 cup dry white wine
2 cups chicken stock
2 dried bay leaves
7 ounces cremini mushrooms
3 tablespoons heavy cream
3 tablespoons whole-grain mustard

1 Preheat oven to 400°F.

2 Wash chicken under cold water; pat dry with paper towels.

3 Heat oil in large ovenproof skillet or Dutch oven. Cook chicken until browned all over. Remove chicken. Cook shallots, carrots and parsnips in same skillet, stirring, 5 minutes or until vegetables are browned lightly.

4 Return chicken to pan with wine, stock and bay leaves; bring to a boil. Cook, covered, in oven 30 minutes. Uncover; cook about 30 minutes or until chicken is cooked through. Add mushrooms; cook, uncovered, about 10 minutes or until mushrooms are tender.

5 Remove chicken and vegetables from skillet; cover to keep warm. Add cream and mustard to skillet; bring to a boil. Boil, uncovered, about 5 minutes or until sauce thickens slightly.

6 Serve chicken with vegetables and mustard cream sauce.

NUTRITIONAL INFO PER SERVING 42g total fat (14g saturated fat);
17g carbohydrate; 47g protein; 7g fiber; 684 calories

braised sweet ginger duck

preparation time 20 minutes **cooking time** 1 hour 50 minutes **serves** 4

4 ½-pound duck

3 cups water

½ cup Chinese cooking wine
  (or dry white wine)

⅓ cup soy sauce

¼ cup firmly packed brown sugar

1 whole star anise

3 green onions, halved

3 cloves garlic, quartered

4-inch piece fresh ginger, unpeeled,
  chopped coarsely

2 teaspoons sea salt

1 teaspoon five-spice powder

1 ¾ pounds baby bok choy, halved

1 Preheat oven to 350°F.

2 Discard neck from duck, wash duck; pat dry with paper towels. Score duck in thickest parts of skin; cut duck in half through breastbone and along both sides of backbone, discard backbone. Tuck wings under duck.

3 Place duck, skin-side down, in medium shallow baking dish; add combined water, wine, soy sauce, sugar, star anise, onions, garlic and ginger. Cover; cook about 1 hour or until duck is cooked to desired degree of doneness.

4 Increase oven temperature to 425°F. Remove duck from braising liquid; strain liquid through cheesecloth-lined sieve into large pot. Place duck, skin-side up, on wire rack in same dish. Rub combined salt and five-spice powder all over duck; roast duck, uncovered, about 30 minutes or until skin is crisp.

5 Skim fat from surface of braising liquid; bring to a boil. Reduce heat; simmer, uncovered, 10 minutes. Add bok choy; simmer, covered, about 5 minutes or until bok choy is just tender.

6 Cut duck halves into two pieces; divide bok choy, braising liquid and duck among plates. Serve with steamed jasmine rice, if desired.

Tip You can ask your butcher to quarter the duck for you.

NUTRITIONAL INFO PER SERVING 106g total fat (32g saturated fat); 18g carbohydrate; 41g protein; 4g fiber; 1190 calories

coq à la bière

preparation time 30 minutes **cooking time** 1 hour 50 minutes **serves** 4

Coq à la bière is a specialty of the beer-producing region of Alsace, in France. This recipe uses a pale ale instead of the traditional dark brew, resulting in a light, delicate sauce that suits the chicken perfectly.

3-pound chicken (cut into pieces)
¼ cup all-purpose flour
1 ½ tablespoons butter
4 large carrots
1 ½ tablespoons olive oil
6 shallots, peeled
3 tablespoons brandy
1 ½ cups pale ale
1 cup chicken stock
1 bay leaf
2 sprigs fresh thyme
2 sprigs fresh flat-leaf parsley
1 ½ tablespoons butter, extra
7 ounces mushrooms
½ cup heavy cream

1 Coat chicken pieces in flour; shake off excess. Melt 1 ½ tablespoons of butter in large pot; cook chicken, in batches, until browned all over.

2 Cut carrots into 2-inch lengths; cut lengths in half lengthwise then cut halves thickly into strips.

3 Heat oil in same cleaned pot; cook shallots, stirring occasionally, 5 minutes or until browned lightly. Add carrots; cook, stirring, 5 minutes. Add brandy; cook, stirring, until liquid evaporates. Add chicken, ale, stock and herbs; bring to a boil. Reduce heat; simmer, uncovered, 1 ¼ hours.

4 Melt 1 ½ tablespoons of butter in medium skillet; cook mushrooms, stirring, until just tender. Add mushrooms and cream to chicken; cook, covered, 15 minutes. Serve coq à la bière with mashed potatoes, if desired.

NUTRITIONAL INFO PER SERVING 55g total fat (24g saturated fat); 14g carbohydrate; 40g protein; 4g fiber; 758 calories

crispy orange duck with spinach rice pilaf

preparation time 15 minutes **cooking time** 30 minutes **serves** 4

2 tablespoons olive oil

2 ounces dried vermicelli or angel hair
   pasta, roughly broken

1 cup long-grain white rice

1 small yellow onion, finely chopped

1 cup vegetable or chicken stock

1 ½ cups water

4 duck breasts (1 ¼ pounds)

¼ cup brown sugar

1 teaspoon grated orange peel

2 tablespoons fresh orange juice

1 fresh red serrano pepper, chopped finely

¾-inch piece fresh ginger, grated

1 tablespoon balsamic vinegar

3 ounces baby spinach

½ cup roasted pine nuts

1 Heat oil in large pot; cook pasta pieces, stirring, about 2 minutes or until golden brown. Add rice and onion; cook, stirring, until onion softens and rice is translucent.

2 Add the stock and water; bring to a boil. Reduce heat, and simmer, covered, about 15 minutes or until liquid is absorbed and rice is just tender.

3 Cook duck, skin-side down, in heated large skillet about 5 minutes or until skin is browned and crisp. Turn duck; cook about 5 minutes or until cooked to desired degree of doneness. Remove from pan, cover, and keep warm.

4 Drain all but 2 tablespoons of duck fat from pan; reheat. Add sugar, orange peel, orange juice, pepper, ginger, and vinegar; bring to a boil. Reduce heat; simmer sauce, uncovered, 2 minutes.

5 Stir spinach and nuts into pilaf; serve with duck topped with sauce.

NUTRITIONAL INFO PER SERVING 79g total fat (19g saturated fat); 65g carbohydrate; 29g protein; 3g fiber; 1083 calories

cashew chicken stir-fry with noodles

preparation time 20 minutes **cooking time** 15 minutes **serves** 6

1 pound Asian stir-fry noodles (udon)

3 tablespoons peanut oil

2 pounds boneless, skinless chicken
   thighs, sliced thinly

1 medium onion, sliced thinly

1 clove garlic, crushed

2 teaspoons grated fresh ginger

1 medium red bell pepper, sliced thinly

1 ½ tablespoons brown sugar

3 tablespoons soy sauce

½ cup teriyaki sauce

1 pound broccoli rabe, chopped coarsely

½ cup unsalted roasted cashews

1 Place noodles in medium heatproof bowl; cover with boiling water, separate with fork, drain.

2 Heat half of the oil in wok or large skillet; stir-fry chicken, in batches, until browned lightly.

3 Heat remaining oil in same wok; stir-fry onion, garlic, ginger and bell pepper about 3 minutes or until onion is just tender.

4 Return chicken to wok with sugar, sauces and broccoli rabe; stir-fry until chicken is cooked through and broccoli rabe is wilted. Add noodles and half of the nuts; toss gently until heated through. Top with remaining nuts.

NUTRITIONAL INFO PER SERVING 22g total fat (6g saturated fat); 28g carbohydrate; 40g protein; 4g fiber; 503 calories

Asian chicken burgers with cucumber salad and wasabi mayo

preparation time 15 minutes (plus refrigeration time) **cooking time** 15 minutes **serves** 4

1 pound ground chicken

1 ½ tablespoons soy sauce

1 egg

1 cup breadcrumbs

1 teaspoon sesame oil

2 green onions, chopped finely

4 hamburger buns

1 cup mixed salad greens

Cucumber salad

1 small cucumber

¼ cup drained pickled ginger

½ cup rice vinegar

1 teaspoon salt

1 ½ tablespoons sugar

Wasabi mayo

¼ cup mayonnaise

2 teaspoons wasabi paste

1 Make cucumber salad and wasabi mayo.

2 Combine chicken, soy sauce, egg, breadcrumbs, oil and onions by hand in large bowl; shape mixture into four burgers.

3 Cook burgers on heated oiled grill pan or skillet, uncovered, about 15 minutes or until cooked through.

4 Split buns in half horizontally; toast, cut-side up. Spread wasabi mayo on buns, followed by greens, burgers and drained cucumber salad.

Cucumber salad Using sharp knife or mandolin, slice cucumber thinly. Combine cucumber with remaining ingredients. Cover; refrigerate 30 minutes.

Wasabi mayo Combine ingredients in small bowl.

NUTRITIONAL INFO PER SERVING 22g total fat (4.8g saturated fat); 58g carbohydrate; 35g protein; 4g fiber; 579 calories

Beef

Everyone's favorite meat, beef can be roasted, grilled, barbecued, pan-fried, stir-fried, stewed or braised. Its strong robust flavor carries piquant sauces and marinades to perfection.

porterhouse steaks with blue cheese mashed potatoes

preparation time 30 minutes **cooking time** 40 minutes **serves** 4

1 ½ tablespoons olive oil

1 ½ tablespoons butter

2 large red onions (about 1 ¼ pounds), sliced thinly

3 tablespoons brown sugar

3 tablespoons balsamic vinegar

4 porterhouse steaks (2 pounds)

½ cup dry red wine

¾ cup chicken stock

½ tablespoons cold butter, chopped

Blue cheese mashed potatoes

2 pounds russet potatoes, chopped coarsely

3 tablespoons butter, softened

¾ cup hot milk

3 ½ ounces firm blue cheese, crumbled

¼ cup coarsely chopped fresh chives

1 Heat oil and butter in large skillet; cook onions, stirring, until onions soften. Add sugar and vinegar; cook, stirring occasionally, about 15 minutes or until onions caramelize. Cover to keep warm.

2 Make blue cheese mashed potatoes.

3 Cook beef, in batches, in heated large, lightly oiled skillet until cooked to desired degree of doneness. Cover beef; let stand 10 minutes.

4 Bring wine to a boil in same skillet; boil, uncovered, until reduced by half. Add stock; return to a boil. Whisk in cold butter, piece by piece, until sauce is smooth.

5 Divide beef, onions and mashed potatoes among serving plates; drizzle with sauce.

Blue cheese mashed potatoes Boil, steam or microwave potatoes until tender, drain. Mash potatoes in large bowl with butter and milk until smooth; fold in cheese and chives. Cover to keep warm.

NUTRITIONAL INFO PER SERVING 54g total fat (28g saturated fat); 43g carbohydrate; 67g protein; 6g fiber; 947 calories

horseradish crusted filet of beef with arugula salad

preparation time 20 minutes (plus refrigeration time) **cooking time** 50 minutes (plus standing time) **serves** 6

¼ cup prepared horseradish

1 ½ tablespoons olive oil

2-pound piece beef tenderloin

3 tablespoons whole-grain mustard

1 ½ tablespoons coarsely chopped
 fresh flat-leaf parsley

½ cup fresh breadcrumbs

1 ½ tablespoons butter, melted

Arugula salad

3 ½ cups baby arugula

1 medium red onion, sliced thinly

8 green onions, sliced thinly

¼ cup toasted pine nuts

⅓ cup balsamic vinegar

⅓ cup olive oil

1 Combine horseradish and oil in large bowl; add beef, turn to coat in mixture. Cover; refrigerate 3 hours or overnight.

2 Sear beef in heated oiled skillet, turning, until browned all over. Reduce heat; cook beef, turning occasionally, about 30 minutes or until cooked. Cover, let stand 10 minutes.

3 Make arugula salad.

4 Preheat broiler.

5 Combine mustard, parsley and breadcrumbs in small bowl with half the butter. Brush beef with remaining butter; press breadcrumb mixture over beef. Broil beef until crust is browned. Let stand 10 minutes; slice thickly. Serve with arugula salad.

Arugula salad Combine ingredients in large bowl.

Tip For this recipe, be sure to use prepared white horseradish, not cream-style horseradish.

NUTRITIONAL INFO PER SERVING 34g total fat (9g saturated fat); 9g carbohydrate; 38g protein; 2g fiber; 498 calories

standing rib roast with roasted vegetables

preparation time 20 minutes **cooking time** 1 hour 30 minutes **serves** 4

2 ½ pounds standing rib roast

¼ cup olive oil

1 teaspoon kosher salt

2 teaspoons cracked black pepper

1 pound new potatoes

1 pound butternut squash,
  chopped coarsely

1 pound sweet potatoes, chopped coarsely

½ cup brandy

1 ½ cups beef stock

1 ½ tablespoons cornstarch

¼ cup water

1 ½ tablespoons finely chopped
  fresh chives

1 Preheat oven to 400°F.

2 Brush roast with 1 ½ tablespoons of the oil; sprinkle with salt and pepper. Heat 1 ½ tablespoons of the oil in large shallow ovenproof skillet; cook roast, uncovered, over high heat until browned all over. Place skillet in oven; roast, uncovered, about 45 minutes or until cooked to desired degree of doneness.

3 Heat remaining oil in another large ovenproof skillet; cook potatoes, stirring, over high heat until browned lightly. Add squash and sweet potatoes, place skillet in oven; roast, uncovered, about 35 minutes or until vegetables are browned.

4 Place roast on vegetables, cover; return to oven to keep warm. Drain juices from roast skillet into medium pot, add brandy; bring to a boil. Add stock and blended cornstarch and water; cook, stirring, until sauce boils and thickens slightly. Stir in chives; pour into serving dish.

5 Serve roast and vegetables on a large platter; accompany with sauce.

NUTRITIONAL INFO PER SERVING 31g total fat (9g saturated fat); 41g carbohydrate; 64g protein; 6g fiber; 770 calories

beef tenderloin with red wine risotto

preparation time 15 minutes **cooking time** 40 minutes (plus standing time) **serves** 4

1-pound piece beef tenderloin
1 ½ tablespoons olive oil
½ teaspoon kosher salt
1 teaspoon ground black pepper
¼ cup dry red wine
½ cup beef stock

Red wine risotto

3 cups vegetable or beef stock
3 tablespoons butter
1 medium onion, chopped finely
1 cup arborio rice
1 cup dry red wine
¼ cup finely grated parmesan cheese
3 green onions, sliced thinly

1 Preheat oven to 400°F.

2 Trim excess fat from tenderloin; tie tenderloin with kitchen string at 1 ¼-inch intervals. Place tenderloin in lightly oiled shallow ovenproof skillet; brush all over with oil, sprinkle with salt and pepper. Roast, uncovered, in oven about 20 minutes or until cooked to desired degree of doneness.

3 Start making red wine risotto.

4 Remove tenderloin from skillet, cover; let stand 10 minutes. Place skillet over low heat, add wine; simmer, stirring, about 2 minutes or until mixture reduces by half. Add stock; stir until sauce comes to a boil. Strain sauce into serving dish. Serve sliced tenderloin with red wine risotto, drizzled with sauce.

Red wine risotto Place stock in medium pot; bring to a boil. Reduce heat; simmer, covered. Heat half of the butter in large pot; cook onion, stirring, until softened. Add rice; stir to coat rice in onion mixture. Add wine; bring to a boil. Reduce heat; simmer, stirring, 2 minutes. Stir in ½ cup of the simmering stock; cook, stirring, over low heat, until liquid is absorbed. Continue adding stock mixture, ½ cup at a time, stirring until absorbed after each addition. Total cooking time should be about 35 minutes or until rice is just tender. Add cheese, remaining butter and green onions, stirring until butter melts.

NUTRITIONAL INFO PER SERVING 23g total fat (11g saturated fat); 44g carbohydrate; 35g protein; 1g fiber; 575 calories

beef tenderloin with
potato pancakes and mushroom cream

preparation time 20 minutes **cooking time** 45 minutes **serves** 4

If crème fraîche isn't available substitute with equal parts sour cream and heavy cream.

3 tablespoons olive oil

1 ¾ pounds beef tenderloin

1 large sweet potato (about 1 pound)

2 large russet potatoes (about 1 ¼ pounds)

6 tablespoons butter

3 tablespoons olive oil

2 tablespoons butter

7 ounces cremini mushrooms, halved

12 ounces oyster mushrooms, halved

7 ounces crème fraîche

3 green onions, sliced thinly

⅓ cup firmly packed fresh flat-leaf parsley

1 Preheat oven to 400°F.

2 Heat 3 tablespoons of olive oil in large shallow ovenproof skillet; sear beef, uncovered, until browned all over. Roast, uncovered, about 35 minutes or until cooked as desired. Cover to keep warm.

3 Coarsely grate sweet potato and russet potatoes into large bowl. Using hands, squeeze out excess moisture from potato mixture; shape mixture into eight portions. Heat 1 tablespoon of the butter and 1 teaspoon of olive oil in medium non-stick skillet; spread one portion of the potato mixture in skillet, flatten with spatula to form a firm pancake-like patty. Cook, uncovered, over medium heat until browned; invert potato cake onto large plate then gently slide back into skillet to cook other side. Drain on paper towels; cover to keep warm. Repeat process with remaining butter, oil and potato mixture.

4 Heat 2 tablespoons of butter in same cleaned skillet; cook mushrooms, stirring, until just tender. Add crème fraîche; bring to a boil. Reduce heat; simmer, stirring, until sauce thickens slightly. Remove from heat; stir in onions and parsley. Serve mushrooms with potato cakes and sliced beef.

NUTRITIONAL INFO PER SERVING 70g total fat (34g saturated fat); 34g carbohydrate; 54g protein; 8g fiber; 976 calories

steaks with herb butter and fries

preparation time 20 minutes (plus standing time) **cooking time** 30 minutes **serves** 4

Our take on a French bistro's steak frites cooks a tender piece of beef to individual perfection and pairs it with freshly made fries and a generous dab of herb butter. The potatoes have been fried twice to guarantee their crispness. We used sirloin with the bone in, but rib eye, filet mignon, or New York strip steaks are all suitable for this recipe.

2 pounds russet or Idaho potatoes

1 ⅓ tablespoons cracked black pepper

2 teaspoons salt

four 8-ounce steaks

peanut oil, for deep-frying

1 ½ tablespoons olive oil

Herb butter

1 clove garlic

5 tablespoons butter, softened

3 tablespoons finely chopped fresh basil

3 tablespoons finely chopped fresh
   flat-leaf parsley

1 Peel potatoes and cut into ¼-inch slices; cut each slice into ¼-inch strips. Place potatoes in large bowl, cover with water; let stand 1 hour. Drain; pat dry with paper towels.

2 Make herb butter.

3 Combine pepper and salt on baking sheet; press both sides of beef into pepper and salt mixture. Let beef rest on baking sheet while making fries.

4 Heat peanut oil in large pot; fry potatoes, in batches, about 3 minutes or until just tender, but not browned. Drain on paper towels.

5 Heat olive oil in large skillet; cook beef until browned on both sides and cooked as desired. Cover; let stand 5 minutes.

6 Reheat oil in pot; fry potatoes again, in batches, until browned lightly and crisp. Drain on paper towels. Season with salt.

7 Divide beef among plates; top with herb butter, serve with fries.

Herb butter Place ingredients in small bowl, beat until combined. Place on piece of plastic wrap, wrap tightly, shape into rectangle; refrigerate until firm.

NUTRITIONAL INFO PER SERVING 57g total fat (21g saturated fat); 27g carbohydrate; 57g protein; 4g fiber; 796 calories

bacon-wrapped filets with red pepper tomato sauce and steak fries

preparation time 20 minutes **cooking time** 40 minutes **serves** 4

4 large potatoes (2 ½ pounds),
  cut into wedges
1 teaspoon crushed red pepper flakes
3 tablespoons olive oil
8 slices bacon
4 filet mignon steaks (1 pound)

Red pepper tomato sauce
2 medium red bell peppers
1 ½ tablespoons olive oil
1 medium onion, chopped coarsely
3 cloves garlic, crushed
14 ½-ounce can crushed tomatoes,
  undrained
1 ½ tablespoons balsamic vinegar

1 Preheat oven to 425°F. Make red pepper tomato sauce.

2 Place potatoes, in single layer, in large shallow baking dish; drizzle with combined red pepper flakes and half of the oil. Roast, uncovered, turning occasionally, about 20 minutes or until browned all over.

3 Wrap two slices bacon around circumference of each steak, trim to fit, secure with toothpick.

4 Heat remaining oil in large heavy-based skillet; cook steak until browned on both sides and cooked to desired degree or doneness.

5 Serve steaks with chili wedges and red pepper tomato sauce.

Red pepper tomato sauce Quarter bell peppers; remove seeds and membranes. Roast bell pepper under broiler or in 475°F oven, skin-side up, until skin blisters and blackens. Cover with plastic wrap or foil for 5 minutes. Peel away skin; chop bell pepper coarsely. Heat oil in medium pot; cook onion and garlic, stirring, until onion softens. Add bell pepper with undrained tomatoes and vinegar; bring to a boil. Reduce heat; simmer, uncovered, stirring occasionally, about 20 minutes or until sauce thickens. Blend or process, in batches, until mixture is pureed.

NUTRITIONAL INFO PER SERVING 31.2g total fat (8.5g saturated fat); 48.5g carbohydrate; 50g protein; 7.9g fiber; 691 calories

chateaubriand

preparation time 45 minutes **cooking time** 50 minutes **serves** 6

Named after the 19th-century author François Chateaubriand, this special-occasion dish has become synonymous with the cut of beef used in its presentation.

2 pounds potatoes
3 tablespoons unsalted butter
¼ cup olive oil
3 tablespoons finely chopped fresh chives
1¾-pound piece beef tenderloin
14 ounces baby vine-ripened tomatoes
14 ounces baby carrots, trimmed
12 ounces broccolini
8 ounces baby yellow squash

Bearnaise sauce

⅓ cup white wine vinegar
½ teaspoon black peppercorns
2 green onions, chopped finely
3 egg yolks
1 stick plus 2 tablespoons unsalted
   butter, melted
2 teaspoons finely chopped fresh tarragon

Mushroom sauce

1 medium onion, chopped finely
5 ounces button mushrooms, quartered
5 ounces oyster mushrooms, sliced thickly
½ cup beef stock
¼ cup dry red wine
¼ cup heavy cream

1 Preheat oven to 425°F.

2 Make bearnaise sauce.

3 Cut potatoes into ½-inch slices. Heat butter and half of the oil in large non-stick skillet; cook potatoes, uncovered, turning occasionally, until browned lightly. Reduce heat; cook potatoes, covered, turning occasionally, about 15 minutes or until tender. Stir in chives.

4 Season beef with salt and pepper. Heat remaining oil in medium ovenproof skillet; sear beef, uncovered, until browned all over. Place skillet in oven; roast beef, uncovered, 10 minutes. Add tomatoes to skillet; roast, uncovered, about 10 minutes or until beef is cooked as desired and tomatoes are soft. Remove beef and tomatoes from skillet; cover to keep warm.

5 Make mushroom sauce, using skillet with beef juices.

6 Boil, steam or microwave carrots, broccolini and squash, separately, until just tender; drain. Serve beef with potatoes and vegetables on large serving platter accompanied with both sauces.

Bearnaise sauce Combine vinegar, peppercorns and onions in small pot; bring to a boil. Reduce heat; simmer, uncovered, about 5 minutes or until liquid has reduced by half. Strain over medium heatproof bowl; discard peppercorns and onions. Whisk yolks into liquid in bowl until combined. Set bowl over medium pot of simmering water; gradually whisk in melted butter in thin, steady stream until mixture thickens slightly. Remove from heat; stir in tarragon. Cover to keep warm.

Mushroom sauce Place same ovenproof skillet with beef juices over medium heat, add onion and mushrooms; cook, stirring, until onion softens. Add stock, wine and cream; bring to a boil. Reduce heat; simmer, uncovered, stirring, about 10 minutes or until sauce thickens slightly and mushrooms are tender. Cover to keep warm.

NUTRITIONAL INFO PER SERVING 47g total fat (24g saturated fat); 27g carbohydrate; 39g protein; 10g fiber; 704 calories

steak sandwich revisited

preparation time 20 minutes **cooking time** 1 hour 20 minutes **serves** 4

4 filet mignon steaks (1 ¾ pounds)
8 thick slices crusty white bread
3 tablespoons olive oil
2 cups arugula, trimmed

Chili tomato spread

1 ½ tablespoons olive oil
2 cloves garlic, crushed
4 medium tomatoes (1 ¾ pounds),
  chopped coarsely
1 ½ tablespoons Worcestershire sauce
½ cup sweet Thai chili sauce
⅓ cup firmly packed brown sugar
1 ½ tablespoons coarsely chopped
  fresh cilantro

Caramelized leeks

2 tablespoons butter
1 medium leek, sliced thinly
3 tablespoons brown sugar
3 tablespoons dry white wine

1 Make chili tomato spread and caramelized leeks.

2 Cook steaks on heated oiled grill or grill pan until browned on both sides and cooked to desired degree of doneness.

3 Brush both sides of bread slices with oil; toast both sides under hot broiler. Layer arugula, steaks, chili tomato spread and caramelized leeks between bread slices.

Chili tomato spread Heat oil in medium pot; cook garlic, stirring, until browned lightly. Add tomatoes, sauces and sugar; bring to a boil. Reduce heat; simmer, uncovered, about 45 minutes or until mixture thickens. Let stand 10 minutes; stir in cilantro.

Caramelized leeks Melt butter in skillet; cook leek, stirring, until softened. Add sugar and wine; cook, stirring occasionally, 20 minutes or until caramelized.

NUTRITIONAL INFO PER SERVING 36g total fat (12g saturated fat); 80g carbohydrate; 54g protein; 9g fiber; 885 calories

beef kabobs two ways with lemon garlic potatoes

preparation time 25 minutes (plus refrigeration time) **cooking time** 30 minutes **serves** 4

Soak 16 small bamboo skewers in cold water for at least one hour before use to prevent them from scorching and splintering.

2 pounds russet or Idaho potatoes

1 ½ tablespoons olive oil

8 ounces ground beef

1 clove garlic, crushed

¼ teaspoon cayenne pepper

1 egg white, beaten lightly

3 tablespoons dried breadcrumbs

14 ounces boneless sirloin steak,
   cut into ¾-inch cubes

1 teaspoon hot paprika

⅓ cup plain or Greek-style yogurt

1 ½ tablespoons coarsely chopped
   fresh cilantro

Lemon garlic dressing

¼ cup fresh lemon juice

2 cloves garlic, crushed

⅓ cup olive oil

2 teaspoons Dijon mustard

1 ½ tablespoons coarsely chopped
   fresh cilantro

1 Preheat oven to 400°F.

2 Scrub unpeeled potatoes, dry with paper towels; quarter lengthwise. Place potatoes, in single layer, in medium baking dish; drizzle with oil. Roast, uncovered, about 30 minutes or until tender.

3 Combine beef, garlic, pepper, egg white and breadcrumbs by hand in medium bowl; shape mixture into eight sausages. Thread one sausage onto each of eight skewers, cover; refrigerate 15 minutes.

4 Thread steak cubes onto eight remaining skewers; sprinkle with paprika. Cook all skewers, in batches, on heated oiled grill or grill pan until browned all over and cooked as desired.

5 Make lemon garlic dressing.

6 Place potatoes and dressing in large serving bowl; toss gently to combine. Combine yogurt and cilantro in small bowl.

7 Serve skewers with potato salad and yogurt mixture.

Lemon garlic dressing Whisk together all ingredients.

NUTRITIONAL INFO PER SERVING 38g total fat (10g saturated fat); 37g carbohydrate; 44g protein; 6g fiber; 670 calories

fajitas with fresh salsa and guacamole

preparation time 25 minutes (plus refrigeration time) **cooking time** 15 minutes **serves** 4

3 tablespoons vegetable oil

⅓ cup fresh lime juice

¼ cup coarsely chopped fresh oregano

2 cloves garlic, crushed

¼ cup coarsely chopped fresh cilantro

2 teaspoons ground cumin

1 ¾ pounds beef skirt steak

1 medium red bell pepper, sliced thickly

1 medium green bell pepper, sliced thickly

1 medium yellow bell pepper, sliced thickly

1 large red onion, sliced thickly

20 small flour tortillas

Fresh salsa

2 cloves garlic, crushed

3 medium tomatoes (about 1 pound),
   seeded, chopped finely

1 small white onion, chopped finely

2 radishes, chopped finely

1 small cucumber, chopped finely

3 tablespoons coarsely chopped
   fresh cilantro

1 jalapeño pepper, chopped finely

3 tablespoons fresh lime juice

Guacamole

2 small avocados

3 tablespoons fresh lime juice

1 Combine oil, lime juice, oregano, garlic, cilantro and cumin in large bowl, add beef; toss beef to coat in marinade. Cover; refrigerate 30 minutes or overnight.

2 Cook beef, bell peppers and onion on heated oiled grill or skillet, uncovered, until beef is cooked to desired degree of doneness and vegetables are just tender. Cover to keep warm.

3 Make fresh salsa and guacamole.

4 Make four stacks of five tortillas each, wrap in aluminum foil; heat on both sides on grill or skillet until tortillas are warm and softened.

5 Cut beef into ¼-inch slices; combine with cooked vegetables. Serve with fresh salsa, guacamole and tortillas.

Fresh salsa Combine ingredients in small bowl.

Guacamole Mash ingredients in small bowl.

NUTRITIONAL INFO PER SERVING 36g total fat (7g saturated fat); 108g carbohydrate; 65g protein; 18g fiber; 1056 calories

barbecued short ribs and potato pancakes

preparation time 25 minutes (plus marinating time) **cooking time** 3 hours 10 minutes **serves** 4

3 tablespoons vegetable oil

1 medium onion, chopped coarsely

3 cloves garlic, crushed

½ cup dry red wine

¼ cup firmly packed brown sugar

3 tablespoons Dijon mustard

3 tablespoons Worcestershire sauce

14 ½-ounce can crushed tomatoes, undrained

4 ½ pounds beef short ribs

Potato pancakes

2 medium potatoes, grated coarsely

⅓ cup self-rising flour

¼ teaspoon ground nutmeg

3 eggs, beaten lightly

½ cup buttermilk

1 ½ tablespoons finely chopped fresh chives

2 egg whites

2 tablespoons butter

1 ½ tablespoons vegetable oil

1 Heat oil in small pot; cook onion and garlic, stirring, until onion softens. Stir in wine, sugar, mustard, Worcestershire sauce and tomatoes; bring to a boil. Reduce heat; simmer barbecue sauce, uncovered, 5 minutes, cool. Reserve half of the barbecue sauce; store, covered, in refrigerator.

2 Using kitchen scissors, separate ribs; place in large bowl with remaining barbecue sauce; toss ribs to coat all over with sauce. Cover; refrigerate 3 hours or overnight.

3 Preheat oven to 275°F.

4 Drain ribs; reserve marinade. Place ribs, in single layer, in large shallow baking dish. Bake, covered, about 1 ½ hours, brushing occasionally with reserved marinade; uncover, bake additional hour or until meat is tender.

5 Heat reserved barbecue sauce; bring to a boil. Reduce heat; simmer, uncovered, about 30 minutes or until sauce thickens. Blend or process sauce until smooth.

6 Serve ribs and potato pancakes, drizzled with hot barbecue sauce.

Potato pancakes Pat grated potatoes with paper towels, until dry. Place flour and nutmeg in medium bowl; gradually whisk in eggs and buttermilk, stir in potatoes and chives. Place egg whites in small bowl; beat with electric mixer until soft peaks form; fold into batter. Heat butter and oil in medium heavy-based skillet; pour approximately ¼-cup amounts of the batter, in batches, into skillet; cook until browned on both sides and tender.

NUTRITIONAL INFO PER SERVING 47g total fat (17g saturated fat); 43g carbohydrate; 91g protein; 4g fiber; 987 calories

hoisin-braised short ribs

preparation time 10 minutes **cooking time** 2 hours 45 minutes **serves** 4

½ cup hoisin sauce

1 cup beef stock

¼ cup firmly packed brown sugar

2-inch piece fresh ginger, grated

2 cloves garlic, crushed

2 star anise

½ cup fresh orange juice

2-inch strip orange peel

1 fresh serrano pepper, chopped coarsely

4 ½ pounds beef short ribs

1 Preheat oven to 300°F.

2 Combine hoisin, stock, sugar, ginger, garlic, star anise, orange juice, peel and pepper in large shallow baking dish, add ribs; turn ribs to coat in mixture. Cover; cook 2 hours.

3 Turn ribs; cook, covered, about another 30 minutes or until ribs are tender. Remove ribs from dish; cover to keep warm.

4 Pour braising liquid into large measuring cup; skim fat from surface. Place liquid in medium pot; bring to a boil. Reduce heat; simmer, uncovered, about 10 minutes or until sauce thickens slightly.

5 Drizzle ribs with sauce; serve with steamed jasmine rice and broccoli rabe, if desired.

Tip Hoisin sauce is a thick, sweet Chinese barbecue sauce found in the Asian food section of most supermarkets.

NUTRITIONAL INFO PER SERVING 28g total fat (12g saturated fat); 30g carbohydrate; 76g protein; 4g fiber; 665 calories

Sri Lankan spicy ribs with coconut pilaf

preparation time 20 minutes (plus refrigeration time) **cooking time** 35 minutes **serves** 4

3 ½ pounds spare ribs

¼ cup peanut oil

¼ cup white vinegar

1 teaspoon Asian chili paste (sambal oelek)

1 teaspoon ground turmeric

4 cloves

½ teaspoon ground cardamom

3 cloves garlic, crushed

2 teaspoons grated fresh ginger

1 small onion, chopped finely

Coconut pilaf

3 tablespoons butter

1 medium onion, chopped coarsely

2 medium carrots, chopped coarsely

2 cups basmati rice, washed, drained

1 quart (4 cups) chicken stock

¼ cup firmly packed fresh cilantro

¼ cup flaked unsweetened coconut

¼ cup raisins

1 Using kitchen scissors, separate ribs into sections; place in large bowl with combined oil, vinegar, chili paste, turmeric, cloves, cardamom, garlic, ginger and onion. Toss ribs to coat all over in marinade, cover; refrigerate 3 hours or overnight.

2 Preheat oven to 475°F.

3 Drain ribs; reserve marinade. Place ribs on wire rack over large shallow baking dish. Roast ribs, uncovered, brushing frequently with reserved marinade, about 30 minutes or until browned and cooked through, turning once halfway through cooking time.

4 Serve ribs on coconut pilaf.

Coconut pilaf Heat butter in medium pot; cook onion and carrots, stirring, until onion softens. Add rice; cook, stirring, 1 minute. Add stock; bring to a boil. Reduce heat; simmer, covered, about 20 minutes or until rice is just tender. Remove from heat; fluff rice with fork. Stir in cilantro, coconut and raisins, cover; let stand 5 minutes before serving.

NUTRITIONAL INFO PER SERVING 30g total fat (129g saturated fat); 92g carbohydrate; 31g protein; 4g fiber; 775 calories

beef bourguignon

preparation time 30 minutes **cooking time** 2 hours 30 minutes **serves** 6

A French classic, this dish was favored dinner-party fare 20 or 30 years ago. Thanks to the resurgence in popularity of rich and rustic comfort food, it has reappeared on restaurant menus and in the repertoire of home cooks.

12 ounces shallots
3 tablespoons olive oil
4 ½ pounds stew beef, trimmed,
   chopped coarsely
2 tablespoons butter
7 slices bacon, chopped coarsely
14 ounces mushrooms, halved
2 cloves garlic, crushed
¼ cup all-purpose flour
1 ¼ cups beef stock
2 ½ cups dry red wine
2 bay leaves
2 sprigs fresh thyme
½ cup coarsely chopped fresh
   flat-leaf parsley

1 Peel shallots, leaving root end intact so shallot remains whole during cooking.
2 Heat oil in large skillet or Dutch oven; cook beef, in batches, until browned. Heat butter in same pan; cook shallots, bacon, mushrooms and garlic, stirring, until shallots are browned lightly.
3 Sprinkle flour over shallot mixture; cook, stirring, until flour mixture thickens and bubbles. Gradually add stock and wine; stir over medium heat until mixture boils and thickens. Return beef and any juices to skillet, add bay leaves and thyme; bring to a boil. Reduce heat; simmer, covered, about 2 hours or until beef is tender, stirring every 30 minutes. (Can be made ahead to this stage. Cover; refrigerate overnight.)
4 Stir in parsley; discard bay leaves just before serving.

NUTRITIONAL INFO PER SERVING 31g total fat (12g saturated fat); 7g carbohydrate; 80g protein; 3g fiber; 636 calories

hearty beef stew with red wine and mushrooms

preparation time 10 minutes **cooking time** 2 hours 50 minutes **serves** 4

The rich combination of stock and wine, plus the long, slow cooking time, gives this stew its robust intensity. Round steak and rump roast are also suitable for this recipe.

3 tablespoons olive oil

3 ½ pounds chuck roast, cut into
   ¾-inch cubes

1 large onion, sliced thickly

2 cloves garlic, crushed

8 ounces mushrooms, quartered

2 celery stalks, sliced thickly

28-ounce can crushed tomatoes

½ cup dry red wine

1 ½ cups beef stock

2 medium potatoes, quartered

4 large carrots, sliced thickly

2 teaspoons coarsely chopped fresh thyme

7 ounces green beans, trimmed

7 ounces yellow beans, trimmed

1 Heat half of the oil in large heavy-based pot; cook beef, in batches, over high heat until browned all over.

2 Heat remaining oil in same pot; cook onion and garlic, stirring, until onion softens. Add mushrooms and celery; cook, stirring, 3 minutes. Return beef to pot with tomatoes, wine and stock; bring to a boil. Reduce heat; simmer, covered, 2 hours.

3 Add potatoes and carrots; simmer, covered, about 30 minutes or until meat is tender. Stir in thyme.

4 Boil, steam or microwave beans until just tender; drain.

5 Serve stew with beans and a warmed loaf of crusty bread.

NUTRITIONAL INFO PER SERVING 33g total fat (11g saturated fat); 27g carbohydrate; 90g protein; 12g fiber; 808 calories

beef, barley and mushroom stew with mashed parsnips

preparation time 35 minutes **cooking time** 2 hours 20 minutes **serves** 4

2 pounds beef chuck roast, cut into
   1 ¼-inch pieces

¼ cup all-purpose flour

3 tablespoons olive oil

1½ tablespoons butter

2 medium onions, chopped finely

3 cloves garlic, crushed

2 medium carrots, chopped finely

1 celery stalk, chopped finely

4 sprigs fresh thyme

1 sprig fresh rosemary

1 bay leaf

½ cup pearl barley

2 cups beef stock

½ cup dry white wine

2 cups water

7 ounces cremini mushrooms, quartered

7 ounces button mushrooms, quartered

Mashed parsnips

2 pounds parsnips, chopped coarsely

¾ cup hot milk

2 cloves garlic, crushed

3 tablespoons softened butter

1 Preheat oven to 325°F.

2 Coat beef in flour; shake off excess. Heat oil in large ovenproof skillet; cook beef, in batches, until browned all over.

3 Melt butter in same skillet; cook onions, garlic, carrots, celery and herbs, stirring, until vegetables soften. Add barley, stock, wine and the water; bring to a boil. Return beef to dish, cover; transfer to oven, cook 1 ½ hours.

4 Stir in mushrooms; cook, uncovered, about 30 minutes or until beef and mushrooms are tender.

5 Make mashed parsnips.

6 Serve stew with parsnips. Sprinkle with fresh thyme.

Mashed parsnips Boil, steam or microwave parsnips until tender; drain. Mash parsnips in medium bowl with milk until smooth; stir in garlic and butter.

NUTRITIONAL INFO PER SERVING 35g total fat (15g saturated fat); 53g carbohydrate; 66g protein; 14g fiber; 811 calories

Tuscan beef stew

preparation time 15 minutes **cooking time** 2 hours 40 minutes **serves** 4

1 ½ tablespoons olive oil

14 ounces green onions

2 pounds chuck roast, cut into
    1 ¼-inch pieces

2 tablespoons butter

3 tablespoons all-purpose flour

2 cups dry red wine

1 cup beef stock

1 cup water

2 cloves garlic, crushed

6 sprigs thyme

2 bay leaves

1 celery stalk, chopped coarsely

1 pound baby carrots, halved

2 cups frozen peas

⅓ cup coarsely chopped fresh
    flat-leaf parsley

1 Heat oil in large heavy-based pot; cook onions, stirring occasionally, about 10 minutes or until browned lightly, remove from pot. Cook beef, in batches, over high heat in same pot, until browned all over.

2 Melt butter in same pot, add flour; cook, stirring, until mixture bubbles and thickens. Gradually stir in the wine, stock and water; stir until mixture boils and thickens. Return steak to pot with garlic, thyme and bay leaves; bring to a boil. Reduce heat; simmer, covered, 1 ½ hours.

3 Add onions to pot with celery and carrots; simmer, covered, 30 minutes. Add peas; simmer, uncovered, until peas are just tender. Stir in parsley. Serve with pasta, if desired.

NUTRITIONAL INFO PER SERVING 23g total fat (10g saturated fat); 16g carbohydrate; 57g protein; 9g fiber; 599 calories

beef and red wine casserole

preparation time 20 minutes **cooking time** 1 hour **serves** 4

2 cups water

2 pounds skirt steak, round steak or
　chuck roast, cut into 1 ¼-inch cubes

2 medium onions, sliced thickly

3 tablespoons olive oil

6 cloves garlic, crushed

2 cups beef stock

2 cups dry red wine

½ cup tomato paste

1 ½ tablespoons finely chopped
　fresh rosemary

1 ½ tablespoons finely chopped
　fresh flat-leaf parsley

1 pound fresh fettucine

1 Combine the water, beef, onions, oil, garlic, stock, wine and tomato paste
in deep 3-quart microwave-safe dish; cook, covered, on high (100%) for
50 minutes, stirring every 15 minutes to ensure beef remains covered with
cooking liquid. Uncover; cook on high (100%) about 10 minutes or until beef
is tender. Stir in herbs.

2 During final 10 minutes of casserole cooking time, cook pasta in large pot of
boiling salted water, uncovered, until just tender; drain.

3 Divide pasta among serving dishes; top with beef casserole.

NUTRITIONAL INFO PER SERVING 16g total fat (4g saturated fat);
52g carbohydrate; 68g protein; 5g fiber; 720 calories

shredded beef with Spanish rice and peas

preparation time 40 minutes **cooking time** 2 hours 50 minutes **serves** 6

In Spanish, this traditional Cuban dish is known as ropa vieja, which translates as "old clothes" because the shredded meat resembles shreds of fabric. This dish is best if made a day ahead so the flavors can develop.

2 quarts (8 cups) water

1 bay leaf

5 cloves garlic, quartered

6 black peppercorns

2 large carrots, chopped coarsely

1 celery stalk, chopped coarsely

3 ⅓ pounds beef skirt or flank steak

2 teaspoons dried oregano

1 ½ tablespoons olive oil

1 medium red bell pepper, sliced thickly

1 medium green bell pepper, sliced thickly

2 medium onions, sliced thickly

14 ½-ounce can whole tomatoes, undrained

1 teaspoon ground cumin

1 cup pimiento-stuffed green olives, halved

¼ cup fresh lemon juice

Sofrito

1 ½ tablespoons olive oil

3 slices bacon, chopped finely

3 cloves garlic, crushed

1 small onion, chopped finely

½ small green bell pepper, chopped finely

1 ½ tablespoons tomato paste

3 tablespoons red wine vinegar

Spanish rice and peas

3 cups water

¼ cup olive oil

2 cups medium-grain white rice

1 cup frozen peas

1 Combine the water, bay leaf, garlic, peppercorns, carrots, celery, beef and 1 teaspoon of the oregano in large deep pot; bring to a boil. Reduce heat; simmer, uncovered, about 2 hours or until beef is tender.

2 Make sofrito.

3 Remove beef from braising liquid. Strain liquid over large bowl; discard solids. Using two forks, shred beef coarsely.

4 Heat oil in same cleaned pot; cook sofrito, bell peppers and onions, stirring, until vegetables soften. Return beef and braising liquid to pan with tomatoes, cumin and remaining oregano; bring to a boil. Reduce heat; simmer, uncovered, 20 minutes. Remove from heat; stir in olives and juice.

5 Make Spanish rice and peas; serve with shredded beef.

Sofrito Heat oil in small skillet; cook bacon, garlic, onion and bell pepper, stirring, until onion softens. Add tomato paste and vinegar; cook, stirring, until vinegar evaporates. Cool 10 minutes; blend or process until smooth.

Spanish rice and peas Combine the water and oil in medium pot; bring to a boil. Stir in rice; cook, uncovered, without stirring, about 10 minutes or until liquid has almost evaporated. Reduce heat; simmer, covered, 5 minutes. Gently stir in peas; simmer, covered, about 5 minutes or until rice and peas are tender.

NUTRITIONAL INFO PER SERVING 26g total fat (6g saturated fat); 63g carbohydrate; 68g protein; 8g fiber; 760 calories

meatloaf with bacon and barbecue glaze

preparation time 20 minutes **cooking time** 50 minutes **serves** 4

1 small red bell pepper

14 ounces ground beef

5 ounces ground sausage

1 medium onion, chopped finely

2 cloves garlic, crushed

¼ cup dried breadcrumbs

1 egg, beaten lightly

½ cup coarsely chopped pitted
   green olives

¼ cup coarsely chopped fresh basil

1 ½ tablespoons coarsely chopped
   fresh oregano

13 slices bacon (1 pound),
   sliced lengthwise

Barbecue glaze

¼ cup water

1 ½ tablespoons tomato paste

1 ½ tablespoons red wine vinegar

3 tablespoons brown sugar

1 Quarter bell pepper; remove and discard seeds and membrane. Roast under broiler or at 475°F, skin-side up, until skin blisters and blackens. Cover bell pepper pieces with plastic wrap or aluminum foil for 5 minutes. Peel away skin; cut bell pepper into thin strips.

2 Preheat oven to 350°F (or reduce oven temperature to 350°F). Line 3- x 10-inch loaf pan with plastic wrap. Lightly oil 10- x 12-inch shallow baking pan.

3 Combine meats, onion, garlic, breadcrumbs, egg, olives, basil and oregano in large bowl. Press half of the meatloaf mixture into pan. Lay bell pepper strips over top, leaving ½-inch border; press remaining meatloaf mixture over bell pepper.

4 Turn loaf pan onto baking pan; remove plastic wrap from meatloaf. Cover top and sides of meatloaf with bacon, overlapping bacon.

5 Bake meatloaf, uncovered, 15 minutes. Make barbecue glaze.

6 Pour off any excess fat from meatloaf, brush with glaze; bake, uncovered, about 25 minutes or until meatloaf is cooked through. Let stand 10 minutes before slicing.

Barbecue glaze Combine ingredients in small pot; bring to a boil. Reduce heat; simmer, uncovered, 5 minutes.

NUTRITIONAL INFO PER SERVING 37g total fat (15g saturated fat); 21g carbohydrate; 56g protein; 3g fibers; 641 calories

beef chow mein

preparation time 30 minutes **cooking time** 20 minutes **serves** 4

1 ½ tablespoons vegetable oil

1 pound ground beef

1 medium onion, chopped finely

2 cloves garlic, crushed

1 ½ tablespoons curry powder

2 large carrots, chopped finely

2 celery stalks, sliced thinly

5 ounces mushrooms, sliced thinly

1 cup chicken stock

⅓ cup oyster sauce

3 tablespoons dark soy sauce

1 pound thin fresh egg noodles

½ cup frozen peas

½ small Chinese cabbage,
   shredded coarsely

1 Heat oil in wok or large skillet; stir-fry beef, onion and garlic until beef is browned. Add curry powder; stir-fry about 1 minute or until fragrant. Add carrots, celery and mushrooms; stir-fry until vegetables soften.

2 Add stock, sauces and noodles; stir-fry 2 minutes. Add peas and cabbage; stir-fry until cabbage just wilts.

NUTRITIONAL INFO PER SERVING 16g total fat (5g saturated fat); 71g carbohydrate; 42g protein; 8g fiber; 615 calories

crispy beef and noodle stir fry

preparation time 15 minutes **cooking time** 15 minutes **serves** 4

If you can't find kecap manis, make your own by heating equal parts soy sauce and brown sugar, stirring until dissolved.

3 tablespoons cornstarch

½ teaspoon baking soda

1 ¼ pounds boneless beef sirloin steak,
   cut into thin strips

⅔ cup peanut oil

3 tablespoons sweet Thai chili sauce

¼ cup kecap manis

1 ½ tablespoons soy sauce

2 teaspoons sesame oil

1 clove garlic, crushed

2 green onions, chopped finely

14 ounces fresh thin egg noodles

7 ounces shiitake mushrooms, quartered

½ small Chinese cabbage,
   shredded coarsely

10 ½ ounces baby bok choy,
   sliced thinly lengthwise

1 Combine cornstarch and baking soda in large bowl. Add beef; toss to coat, shaking off excess.

2 Heat a third of the peanut oil in wok or large skillet; stir-fry about a third of the beef until crisp. Drain on paper towels, cover to keep warm; repeat with remaining peanut oil and beef.

3 Combine sauces, sesame oil, garlic and onion in small bowl.

4 Place noodles in large heatproof bowl, cover with boiling water; separate with fork, drain.

5 Reheat same cleaned wok; stir-fry mushrooms about 2 minutes or until just tender. Add cabbage and bok choy; stir-fry 1 minute. Add sauce mixture, noodles and beef; stir-fry until heated through.

NUTRITIONAL INFO PER SERVING 51g total fat (12g saturated fat); 61g carbohydrate; 48g protein; 6g fiber; 900 calories

beef and eggplant bake with polenta crust

preparation time 20 minutes (plus standing time) **cooking time** 1 hour 20 minutes **serves** 6

2 medium eggplants (about 1 ¼ pounds),
  sliced thickly
3 tablespoons kosher salt
1½ tablespoons olive oil
1 medium onion, chopped coarsely
1 medium red bell pepper,
  chopped coarsely
1 clove garlic, crushed
1 pound ground beef
3 tablespoons tomato paste
½ cup dry red wine
14 ½-ounce can whole tomatoes,
  undrained
1 cup firmly packed fresh basil
1 ½ tablespoons fresh oregano
2 cups chicken stock
2 cups milk
1 cup polenta
1 ½ cups coarsely grated
  mozzarella cheese

1 Place eggplants in colander, sprinkle all over with salt; let stand 30 minutes. Rinse eggplants; drain on paper towels.

2 Heat oil in medium skillet; cook onion, bell pepper and garlic, stirring, until onion softens. Add beef; cook, stirring, until beef changes color. Add tomato paste; cook, stirring, 2 minutes. Add wine; cook, stirring, 5 minutes. Add tomatoes; bring to a boil. Reduce heat; simmer, uncovered, stirring occasionally, about 15 minutes or until liquid is almost evaporated. Chop about a quarter of the basil leaves coarsely; stir into sauce with oregano.

3 Preheat oven to 400°F.

4 Cook eggplants on heated oiled grill pan or skillet until browned.

5 Combine stock and milk in medium pot; bring to a boil. Gradually add polenta, stirring constantly. Reduce heat; simmer, stirring, about 10 minutes or until polenta thickens.

6 Arrange half of the eggplant in shallow 3-quart baking dish; top with half of the beef mixture. Top with remaining eggplant then remaining beef mixture and basil. Spread polenta over basil; sprinkle with cheese. Cook, uncovered, about 20 minutes or until top is browned lightly. Let stand 10 minutes before serving.

Tip Letting the salted eggplant stand for several minutes draws out the bitter liquid in the vegetable. Be sure to rinse the eggplant slices in cold water and pat dry before cooking.

NUTRITIONAL INFO PER SERVING 20g total fat (9g saturated fat); 13g carbohydrate; 29g protein; 12g fiber; 373 calories

Veal

A tender, fine-grained meat with a delicate flavor, veal lends itself beautifully to light sauces and simple accompaniments.

wiener schnitzel with lemon spaetzle

preparation time 20 minutes (plus refrigeration time) **cooking time** 20 minutes **serves** 4

Spaetzle are tiny noodle-like dumplings made by pushing a batter through the holes of a colander or strainer into a pan of boiling water or stock. They are a traditional side dish with weiner schnitzel.

½ cup all-purpose flour
3 eggs, beaten lightly
3 tablespoons milk
2 cups plus ¾ cup dried breadcrumbs
½ cup finely grated parmesan cheese
8 veal cutlets (1 ¾ pounds)
vegetable oil, for shallow-frying

Lemon spaetzle
2 cups all-purpose flour
4 eggs, beaten lightly
½ cup water
2 teaspoons finely grated lemon peel
3 tablespoons butter, chopped

1 Whisk flour, eggs and milk in medium shallow bowl; combine breadcrumbs and cheese in another medium shallow bowl. Coat cutlets, one at a time, in flour mixture then in breadcrumb mixture. Place, in single layer, on baking sheet. Cover; refrigerate 15 minutes.

2 Make lemon spaetzle.

3 Heat oil in large skillet; cook cutlets, in batches, until browned on both sides and cooked through.

4 Serve schnitzel with lemon spaetzle.

Lemon spaetzle Place flour in large bowl, make well in center. Gradually add the eggs and water, stirring, until batter is smooth. Stir in lemon peel. Pour half of the batter into metal colander set over large pot of boiling water; using wooden spoon, push batter through holes of colander, remove colander. When water returns to a boil, boil, uncovered, about 2 minutes or until spaetzle float to the surface. Use slotted spoon to remove spaetzle; drain, place in large bowl. Add half of the butter; toss spaetzle gently until butter melts. Keep warm; repeat with remaining batter and butter.

NUTRITIONAL INFO PER SERVING 43g total fat (14g saturated fat); 105g carbohydrate; 78g protein; 6g fiber; 1136 calories

veal parmesan

preparation time 15 minutes **cooking time** 20 minutes **serves** 4

¼ cup all-purpose flour

2 eggs, beaten lightly

3 tablespoons milk

½ cup corn flake crumbs

½ cup breadcrumbs

4 veal cutlets (8 ounces)

¼ cup olive oil

1 medium onion, chopped finely

2 cloves garlic, crushed

½ cup dry red wine

1 ½ cups bottled pasta sauce

1 cup mozzarella cheese

7 ounces green beans, trimmed

1 pound asparagus, trimmed

1 Preheat oven to 400°F.

2 Combine flour, egg and milk in medium bowl; combine corn flake crumbs and breadcrumbs in another medium bowl. Coat veal, one piece at a time, first in egg mixture then in breadcrumb mixture.

3 Heat 3 tablespoons of the oil in large skillet; cook veal until browned lightly on both sides. Place in lightly greased baking dish.

4 Heat remaining oil in same cleaned skillet; cook onion and garlic, stirring, until onion softens. Add wine; bring to a boil. Boil, stirring, 1 minute. Stir in sauce; bring to a boil. Reduce heat; simmer, uncovered, about 5 minutes or until sauce thickens slightly. Cool 5 minutes.

5 Spoon sauce over each piece of veal; top with cheese. Cook, uncovered, in oven about 15 minutes or until cheese melts and veal is heated through.

6 Boil, steam or microwave beans and asparagus, separately, until just tender; drain. Serve with veal.

NUTRITIONAL INFO PER SERVING 25g total fat (7g saturated fat); 46g carbohydrate; 40g protein; 7g fiber; 604 calories

veal scaloppine with potato-fennel gratin

preparation time 30 minutes **cooking time** 1 hour 5 minutes **serves** 4

14 ounces Yukon Gold potatoes

1 small fennel bulb, sliced thinly

3 teaspoons all-purpose flour

1 ½ cups heavy cream

3 tablespoons milk

1 ½ tablespoons butter, chopped

⅓ cup freshly grated parmesan cheese

½ cup breadcrumbs

3 tablespoons olive oil

1 ¾ pounds veal scaloppine

3 tablespoons fresh lemon juice

¼ cup dry white wine

1 clove garlic, crushed

¾ cup chicken stock

1 teaspoon Dijon mustard

3 tablespoons drained baby capers, rinsed

¼ cup coarsely chopped fresh
   flat-leaf parsley

1 Preheat oven to 350°F. Grease a deep 4-cup baking dish.

2 Using sharp knife or mandolin, cut potatoes into very thin slices; pat dry with paper towels. Layer a third of the potatoes into dish; top with half of the fennel. Continue layering remaining potatoes and fennel, finishing with potatoes.

3 Blend flour with a little of the cream in medium measuring cup to form a smooth paste; stir in milk and remaining cream. Pour heavy cream mixture over potato; dot with butter. Cover with aluminum foil; bake about 45 minutes or until vegetables are just tender. Remove aluminum foil, top with combined cheese and breadcrumbs; bake, uncovered, about 20 minutes or until top is browned lightly.

4 During last 15 minutes of gratin cooking time, heat oil in large skillet; cook veal, in batches, until cooked to desired degree of doneness. Cover to keep warm.

5 Add lemon juice, wine and garlic to same skillet; bring to a boil. Reduce heat; simmer, uncovered, until liquid reduces by half. Add stock and mustard; simmer, uncovered, 5 minutes. Remove from heat; stir in capers and parsley. Serve veal topped with sauce and accompanied by gratin.

Tip We used the creamy, all-purpose Yukon Gold potato in this gratin but you can substitute Idaho, russet, or any good baking potato. Don't peel or slice the potatoes until you're ready to assemble the dish, and make sure you pat the slices dry with paper towels.

NUTRITIONAL INFO PER SERVING 49g total fat (25g saturated fat); 23g carbohydrate; 52g protein; 3g fiber; 745 calories

veal chops with rosemary and arugula pesto

preparation time 15 minutes **cooking time** 1 hour 5 minutes (plus standing time) **serves** 4

2 pounds new potatoes

1 clove garlic, quartered

2 cups baby arugula

¼ cup extra virgin olive oil

¼ cup coarsely chopped fresh rosemary

2 pounds veal rack (8 chops)

½ cup finely grated parmesan cheese

1 ½ tablespoons all-purpose flour

¾ cup beef stock

¼ cup dry white wine

1 ½ tablespoons red currant preserves

1 pound asparagus, trimmed

1 Preheat oven to 400°F.

2 Place potatoes in lightly oiled shallow medium baking dish; roast, uncovered, about 50 minutes or until tender.

3 Blend or process garlic, arugula, oil and 3 tablespoons of the rosemary until mixture forms a paste. Stir remaining rosemary into pesto.

4 Place veal rack on wire rack over large shallow ovenproof skillet; coat veal with pesto. Roast, uncovered, about 40 minutes or until veal is browned and cooked to desired degree of doneness. Remove veal from skillet; cover to keep warm.

5 When potatoes are tender, sprinkle with cheese; roast, uncovered, about 5 minutes or until cheese melts.

6 Place skillet holding veal juices over medium heat, add flour; cook, stirring, until mixture thickens and bubbles. Gradually add stock, wine and preserves, stirring, until sauce boils and thickens slightly.

7 Boil, steam or microwave asparagus until just tender; drain.

8 Slice veal into chops, serve with potatoes, asparagus and sauce.

NUTRITIONAL INFO PER SERVING 22g total fat (5g saturated fat); 41g carbohydrate; 58g protein; 7g fiber; 621 calories

veal loin with figs and port sauce

preparation time 10 minutes (plus marinating time) **cooking time** 50 minutes **serves** 6

This cut of veal includes the tenderloin of veal, which is very pale in color (almost white), is trimmed of any excess fat and has a firm, velvety texture. This dish is also delicious with pork.

1 ¾-pound piece boneless
   loin of veal roast
¼ cup balsamic vinegar
3 tablespoons olive oil
1 clove garlic, crushed
9 medium fresh figs, halved
1 quart (4 cups) water
3 cups milk
1 ½ cups instant polenta
3 tablespoons butter
½ cup heavy cream
4 green onions, chopped finely
½ cup coarsely chopped fresh
   flat-leaf parsley
⅓ cup port
1 cup beef stock
1 ½ tablespoons cornstarch
¼ cup water

1 Place veal in large bowl with combined vinegar, oil and garlic; coat veal all over in marinade. Cover; refrigerate 3 hours or overnight.

2 Preheat oven to 400°F.

3 Drain veal; discard marinade. Heat large ovenproof skillet; cook veal, uncovered, until browned all over. Roast, uncovered, in oven 30 minutes. Stir in fig halves; roast, uncovered, about 10 minutes or until figs are just tender.

4 Combine the water and milk in large pot; bring to a boil. Add polenta in a slow, steady stream, stirring constantly. Reduce heat; simmer, stirring constantly, about 20 minutes or until polenta thickens. Stir in butter, cream, onions and parsley.

5 Remove veal and figs from skillet; cover to keep warm. Place skillet with pan juices over high heat, add port; bring to a boil. Cook, stirring, 2 minutes. Add stock; bring to a boil. Cook, uncovered, 3 minutes. Add blended cornstarch and ¼ cup water; cook, stirring, until sauce boils and thickens.

6 Serve veal on polenta, topped with figs and drizzle with sauce.

NUTRITIONAL INFO PER SERVING 29g total fat (14g saturated fat); 47g carbohydrate; 40g protein; 4g fiber; 628 calories

veal medallions with poivrade sauce and potato gratin

preparation time 30 minutes **cooking time** 1 hour 20 minutes (plus standing time) **serves** 6

2 ½ pounds veal cutlets or scaloppine

3 tablespoons butter

2 shallots, chopped finely

1 large carrot, chopped finely

1 celery stalk, chopped finely

1 clove garlic, crushed

3 tablespoons black peppercorns, crushed

1 ½ tablespoons all-purpose flour

3 tablespoons red wine vinegar

1 cup dry red wine

2 cups beef stock

3 tablespoons red currant preserves

Potato gratin

1 ¾ cups heavy cream

¾ cup milk

2 cloves garlic, crushed

2 pounds Yukon gold or red potatoes,
  cut into ⅛-inch slices

1 medium onion, sliced thinly

3 tablespoons finely grated
  parmesan cheese

1 Make potato gratin.

2 Trim veal fillets; chop trimmings coarsely. Cut each fillet on the diagonal into nine slices; press with side of heavy knife or meat mallet to flatten.

3 Melt half of the butter in medium pot; cook veal trimmings with shallots, carrot, celery, garlic and pepper, stirring, until onions soften. Add flour; cook, stirring, until mixture bubbles and thickens. Add vinegar; cook, stirring, until absorbed. Gradually add wine and stock; stir until mixture boils and thickens. Reduce heat, simmer, uncovered, until sauce is reduced to about 1 ½ cups. Strain into small bowl; discard solids. Return sauce to same cleaned pot; whisk in preserves and remaining butter until sauce is smooth.

4 Cook veal in large lightly oiled skillet, in batches, about 45 seconds on each side or until cooked to desired degree of doneness. Divide potato gratin among serving plates; top with veal medallions, drizzled with sauce.

Potato gratin Preheat oven to 400°F. Combine cream, milk and garlic in small pot; bring to a boil. Combine potatoes with cream mixture in large bowl; layer half of the potato mixture in greased deep 8-inch-square pan. Layer with onion then layer with remaining potato, sprinkle with cheese. Cover with aluminum foil; cook 1 hour. Remove aluminum foil; cook about 20 minutes or until potatoes are tender and top is lightly browned. Let stand 20 minutes before cutting.

Tip Slice potatoes on a mandoline for consistent thickness.

NUTRITIONAL INFO PER SERVING 42g total fat (26g saturated fat); 32g carbohydrate; 54g protein; 4g fiber; 752 calories

veal goulash with braised red cabbage

preparation time 20 minutes **cooking time** 1 hour 30 minutes **serves** 4

1 ½ tablespoons olive oil

1 medium onion, sliced thickly

1 medium red bell pepper, sliced thickly

2 cloves garlic, crushed

1 ¾ pounds boneless veal leg, cut into
   1 ¼-inch cubes

1 ½ tablespoons sweet paprika

½ teaspoon cayenne pepper

14 ½-ounce can crushed tomatoes,
   undrained

1 ½ cups beef stock

1 cup long-grain brown rice

2 tablespoons butter

14 ounces red cabbage, chopped coarsely

1 Heat oil in large pot; cook onion, bell pepper and garlic until onion softens. Add veal, paprika, pepper, undrained tomatoes and ½ cup of the stock; bring to a boil, stirring. Reduce heat; simmer, uncovered, about 1 hour or until veal is tender and sauce thickens slightly.

2 Cook rice in medium pot of boiling water until just tender; drain.

3 Melt butter in large skillet; cook cabbage, stirring, about 5 minutes or until just softened. Add remaining stock; bring to a boil. Reduce heat; simmer, covered, 10 minutes.

4 Serve goulash with rice and braised red cabbage.

NUTRITIONAL INFO PER SERVING 16g total fat (6g saturated fat); 50g carbohydrate; 54g protein; 8g fiber; 575 calories

osso buco

preparation time 45 minutes **cooking time** 2 hours 35 minutes **serves** 6

Ask your butcher to cut the veal into fairly thick (about 1 ½-inch) pieces.

12 pieces veal osso buco (5 ½ pounds)
¼ cup all-purpose flour
¼ cup olive oil
3 tablespoons butter
1 medium onion, chopped coarsely
2 cloves garlic, crushed
3 celery stalks, chopped coarsely
4 large carrots, chopped coarsely
4 medium tomatoes (about 1 ¼ pounds),
    chopped coarsely
3 tablespoons tomato paste
1 cup dry white wine
1 cup beef stock
14 ½-ounce can crushed tomatoes,
    undrained
3 sprigs fresh thyme
¼ cup coarsely chopped fresh
    flat-leaf parsley

Gremolata
1 ½ tablespoons finely grated lemon peel
⅓ cup finely chopped fresh flat-leaf parsley
2 cloves garlic, chopped finely

1 Toss veal and flour together, in batches, in paper or plastic bag; remove veal from bag, shake away excess flour.
2 Heat oil in large skillet or pot; cook veal, in batches, until browned all over.
3 Melt butter in same skillet; cook onion, garlic, celery and carrots, stirring, until vegetables soften. Stir in tomatoes, tomato paste, wine, stock, crushed tomatoes and herbs.
4 Return veal to skillet, fitting pieces upright and tightly together in a single layer; bring to a boil. Cover, reduce heat; simmer 1 ¾ hours. Uncover; cook 30 minutes. (Can be made ahead to this stage. Cover; refrigerate overnight.)
5 Make gremolata.
6 Remove veal from skillet; cover to keep warm. Bring sauce to a boil; boil, uncovered, about 10 minutes or until sauce thickens slightly.
7 Divide veal among serving plates; top with sauce, sprinkle with gremolata. Serve with mashed potatoes or soft polenta, if desired.
Gremolata Combine ingredients in small bowl. Cover with plastic wrap and refrigerate until needed.

NUTRITIONAL INFO PER SERVING 16g total fat (5g saturated fat); 12g carbohydrate; 62g protein; 5g fiber; 479 calories

veal braciole with rice and peas

preparation time 25 minutes **cooking time** 40 minutes **serves** 4

The Italian veal cut known as braciole is similar to a thin cutlet from the leg. In some parts of Italy, when a braciole is filled and rolled, it is known as an involtino.

8 slices pancetta (4 ounces)
8 veal cutlets or scaloppine (1 ¾ pounds)
⅔ cup drained sun-dried tomatoes in oil, sliced thinly
⅓ cup pitted green olives, sliced thinly
1 ½ tablespoons drained baby capers, rinsed
2 teaspoons fresh marjoram
1 ½ tablespoons olive oil

Rice and peas
1 quart (4 cups) water
2 cups chicken stock
3 tablespoons butter
2 cups arborio rice
1 cup frozen peas
1 cup finely grated parmesan cheese
¼ cup finely chopped fresh flat-leaf parsley

1 Preheat oven to 350°F.

2 Place one slice of pancetta on each cutlet; divide tomatoes, olives, capers and marjoram among the cutlets.

3 Roll veal to enclose filling; tie with kitchen string to secure.

4 Start making rice and peas.

5 Heat oil in large skillet; cook braciole, uncovered, until browned all over. Place on baking sheet; bake, uncovered, in oven about 10 minutes or until cooked through.

6 Serve braciole with rice and peas.

Rice and peas Place the water and stock in medium pot; bring to a boil. Reduce heat; simmer, covered. Melt butter in large pot, add rice; stir until rice is coated in butter and slightly opaque. Stir in 1 cup of the hot stock mixture; cook, stirring, over low heat, until liquid is absorbed. Continue adding stock mixture, one cup at a time, stirring until absorbed after each addition. Add peas with last cup of stock mixture; stir in cheese and parsley.

NUTRITIONAL INFO PER SERVING 30g total fat (13.2g saturated fat); 93.8g carbohydrate; 70.7g protein; 6.6g fiber; 946 calories

veal chops with roasted pumpkin risotto

preparation time 30 minutes (plus refrigeration time) **cooking time** 5 hours 30 minutes **serves** 6

If you don't have time to make veal stock, you can substitute 3 cups of beef or chicken stock plus 3 cups of water.

Veal stock

2 pounds veal shank, cut into pieces
1 medium onion, chopped coarsely
1 trimmed celery stalk, chopped coarsely
2 medium carrots, chopped coarsely
2 bay leaves
1 teaspoon black peppercorns
4 quarts (16 cups) water

2 cloves garlic, crushed
3 tablespoons finely chopped
  fresh rosemary
3 tablespoons whole-grain mustard
1 ½ tablespoons olive oil
2 ½ pounds veal rack (6-chop)

Roast pumpkin risotto

1 pound pumpkin or butternut squash,
  chopped coarsely
3 tablespoons olive oil
1 medium onion, chopped finely
1 ½ cups arborio rice
½ cup dry white wine
¼ cup finely grated parmesan cheese
1 ½ tablespoons butter
⅓ cup finely chopped fresh flat-leaf parsley

1 Preheat oven to 425°F; make veal stock. (Can be made ahead to this stage. Cover; refrigerate overnight.)

2 Preheat oven to 350°F.

3 Combine garlic, rosemary, mustard and oil in small bowl. Place veal rack on wire rack over large shallow baking dish; spread garlic mixture over veal rack. Roast, covered, 1 hour. Uncover; roast 30 minutes or until cooked to desired degree of doneness. Cover; let stand 10 minutes.

4 Make roast pumpkin risotto.

5 Slice veal into chops, serve with risotto.

Veal stock Place veal shanks and onion in baking dish; roast, uncovered, about 1 hour or until bones are well browned. Transfer bones and onions to large pot with celery, carrots, bay leaves, peppercorns and the water; bring to a boil. Reduce heat; simmer, uncovered, 3 hours. Strain stock through cheesecloth-lined sieve or colander into bowl; discard solids. Allow stock to cool, cover; refrigerate until cold.

Roast pumpkin risotto About 45 minutes into veal roasting time, place pumpkin on baking sheet; drizzle with half of the oil. Roast, uncovered, with veal about 45 minutes or until browned and tender. Meanwhile, skim fat from surface of stock; place stock in large pot, bring to a boil. Reduce heat; simmer, covered. Heat remaining oil in large pot; cook onion, stirring, until soft. Add rice; stir to coat in onion mixture. Stir in wine; cook, stirring, until liquid is absorbed. Add ½ cup of the simmering stock; cook, stirring, over low heat until stock is absorbed. Continue adding stock, ½ cup at a time, stirring, until stock is absorbed after each addition. Total cooking time should be about 35 minutes or until rice is tender. Just before serving, stir roasted pumpkin, cheese, butter and parsley into risotto.

NUTRITIONAL INFO PER SERVING 18g total fat (5g saturated fat); 47g carbohydrate; 68g protein; 3g fiber; 646 calories

Pork

Pork cuts are quite lean these days, so the flesh dries out easily if cooked over too high a heat. For tender, juicy results every time, cook pork on moderately low heat.

pork chops with stuffed apples and peppercorn cider sauce

preparation time 20 minutes **cooking time** 1 hour **serves** 4

3 tablespoons butter

1 small onion, chopped finely

1 clove garlic, crushed

2 slices bacon, chopped finely

¼ cup breadcrumbs

2 pitted prunes, chopped finely

3 tablespoons finely chopped fresh chives

2 large apples

¾ tablespoon butter, extra

4 pork cutlets (2 pounds)

½ cup apple cider

2 teaspoons drained green peppercorns, crushed

1 ½ cups heavy cream

1 Preheat oven to 350°F.

2 Melt butter in large skillet; cook onion, garlic and bacon, stirring, until onion softens. Stir in breadcrumbs, prunes and half of the chives.

3 Core apples; pierce apples in several places with fork. Press breadcrumb mixture into apple centers; place in large deep ovenproof skillet. Melt extra butter; brush all over apples. Bake, uncovered, 30 minutes.

4 Oil same cleaned skillet; cook pork, uncovered, about 2 minutes on each side or until browned. Place pork in same skillet with apples; cover with aluminum foil. Transfer to oven; cook with apples about 15 minutes or until pork is cooked to desired degree of doneness.

5 Remove pork and apples from skillet; cover to keep warm. Stir cider and peppercorns into juices in skillet; cook, stirring, 1 minute. Add cream; bring to a boil. Reduce heat; simmer, uncovered, until sauce thickens slightly. Stir in remaining chives. Halve apples; serve with pork, drizzle with sauce and serve with mashed potatoes, if desired.

NUTRITIONAL INFO PER SERVING 47g total fat (30g saturated fat); 21g carbohydrate; 36g protein; 3g fiber; 649 calories

pork tenderloin with cranberry stuffing and red wine sauce

preparation time 20 minutes **cooking time** 20 minutes **serves** 4

1 tablespoon olive oil

1 medium yellow onion, chopped finely

1 clove garlic, crushed

2 tablespoons dried cranberries

2 ounces baby spinach

½ cup breadcrumbs

¼ cup toasted pine nuts

1 ¼ pound pork tenderloin

½ cup dry red wine

¾ cup chicken stock

2 tablespoons red currant jelly

1 Heat oil in large skillet; cook onion and garlic, stirring, until onion softens. Add cranberries and spinach; cook, stirring, until spinach wilts. Combine mixture with breadcrumbs and nuts in medium bowl. Cover, and keep warm.

2 Add pork to same skillet; cook, uncovered, until desired degree of doneness. Cover; let stand 5 minutes, and slice into thick pieces.

3 Bring wine to a boil in small pan. Reduce heat; simmer, uncovered, until reduced by half. Add stock and jelly; cook, uncovered, about 10 minutes, stirring occasionally, or until sauce thickens.

4 Top pork with cranberry stuffing; drizzle with sauce.

NUTRITIONAL INFO PER SERVING 15.6g total fat (2.4g saturated fat); 22.2g carbohydrate; 37.1g protein; 2.6g fiber; 404 calories

barbecued ribs

preparation time 25 minutes (plus refrigeration time) **cooking time** 2 hours 10 minutes **serves** 8

7 ¾ pounds pork spare ribs

Barbecue sauce
2 ¼ cups tomato sauce
1 ½ cups apple cider vinegar
⅓ cup olive oil
½ cup Worcestershire sauce
¾ cup firmly packed brown sugar
⅓ cup yellow mustard
1 ½ teaspoons cracked black pepper
3 fresh red serrano or jalapeño peppers, chopped finely
3 cloves garlic, crushed
¼ cup lemon juice

1 Make barbecue sauce.

2 Place slabs of ribs in large deep baking dish; brush both sides of each slab with sauce. Pour remaining sauce over slabs, cover; refrigerate overnight, if possible, turning occasionally.

3 Preheat oven to 325°F.

4 Drain slabs, reserving sauce. Divide slabs of ribs between two wire racks over two large shallow baking dishes. Roast, covered, 1 ½ hours, uncovering to brush with sauce every 20 minutes. Turn slabs midway through cooking time.

5 Increase oven temperature to 425°F. Uncover slabs; bake, brushing frequently with sauce, until slabs are browned and cooked through, turning after 15 minutes.

6 Place remaining barbecue sauce in small pot; bring to a boil. Reduce heat; simmer, stirring, about 4 minutes or until sauce thickens slightly. Using scissors, cut slabs in portions of two or three ribs; serve ribs with hot barbecue sauce.

Barbecue sauce Combine ingredients in medium pot; bring to a boil. Remove from heat; cool.

Tip For easy clean up, line the bottoms of the baking dishes with parchment paper or aluminum foil.

NUTRITIONAL INFO PER SERVING 13g total fat (2g saturated fat); 42g carbohydrate; 47g protein; 2g fiber; 477 calories

margarita marinated pork chops with orange watercress salad

preparation time 15 minutes (plus refrigeration time) **cooking time** 15 minutes **serves** 4

¼ cup fresh lime juice

2 fresh small red serrano or jalapeño peppers, seeded, chopped finely

2 cloves garlic, crushed

½ cup orange marmalade

⅓ cup finely chopped fresh cilantro

½ cup tequila

8 bone-in pork loin chops (5 pounds)

Orange watercress salad

2 large oranges (about 1 ¼ pounds)

¼ cup fresh lime juice

¼ cup orange marmalade

3 tablespoons olive oil

2 teaspoons tequila

3 cups watercress, trimmed

1 medium avocado, sliced thinly

½ cup loosely packed fresh cilantro

1 Combine lime juice, chili, garlic, marmalade, cilantro and tequila, add pork; toss pork to coat in marinade. Cover; refrigerate one hour to overnight.

2 Make orange watercress salad.

3 Drain pork; reserve marinade. Cook pork on heated grill pan or skillet, uncovered, brushing occasionally with marinade, until cooked to desired degree of doneness. Serve pork with salad.

Orange watercress salad Segment oranges over large bowl to reserve juice; stir in lime juice, marmalade and oil. Add remaining ingredients; toss gently to combine.

NUTRITIONAL INFO PER SERVING 58g total fat (17g saturated fat); 68g carbohydrate; 69g protein; 4g fiber; 1155 calories

apple-stuffed pork loin with braised red cabbage

preparation time 1 hour **cooking time** 2 hours 15 minutes **serves** 8

5 ½ pounds boneless pork loin, butterflied

3 tablespoons kosher salt

3 cups apple cider

½ cup chicken stock

3 teaspoons sugar

Apple stuffing

2 tablespoons butter

3 large Granny Smith apples
   (about 1 ¼ pounds), peeled,
   cored, cut into thin wedges

1 medium leek, sliced thinly

1 medium onion, sliced thinly

½ teaspoon ground cinnamon

3 tablespoons sugar

1 cup dried breadcrumbs

1 ½ tablespoons finely grated lemon peel

1 cup coarsely chopped fresh
   flat-leaf parsley

Braised red cabbage

3 tablespoons butter

¼ teaspoon caraway seeds

4 sprigs thyme

1 bay leaf

1 medium onion, chopped finely

1 medium Granny Smith apple, peeled,
   grated coarsely

3 ⅓ pounds red cabbage, sliced thinly

½ cup red wine vinegar

1 ¼ cups water

1 Preheat oven to 475°F.

2 Place pork on cutting board, rind-side up. Run sharp knife about ¼-inch under rind, gradually lifting rind away from pork. Place rind in large shallow baking dish. Using sharp knife, make shallow cuts in one direction diagonally across fat at 1 ¼-inch intervals, then shallow-cut in opposite direction, forming diamonds; rub with salt. Roast, uncovered, about 30 minutes or until crackling is browned and crisp. Chop crackling into serving pieces; reserve.

3 Reduce oven temperature to 350°F. Meanwhile, make apple stuffing.

4 If pork has not been butterflied, slice through the thickest part of pork horizontally without cutting all the way through. Open pork out to form one large piece; press stuffing against the loin along length of pork. Roll pork to enclose stuffing; secure with kitchen string at one-inch intervals.

5 Place pork on rack in large shallow baking dish; pour 2 ½ cups of the cider into dish. Roast, uncovered, about 1 ½ hours or until cooked through.

6 Make braised red cabbage.

7 Remove pork from baking dish; cover to keep warm. Combine juices from baking dish with stock, sugar and remaining cider in a skillet over medium heat; cook, stirring, until sauce thickens slightly.

8 Serve pork, braised red cabbage and crackling drizzled with sauce.

Apple stuffing Heat butter in large skillet; cook apples, leek, onion, cinnamon and sugar, stirring, until leeks and onion soften. Remove from heat; stir in breadcrumbs, lemon peel and parsley.

Braised red cabbage Place butter, caraway seeds, thyme and bay leaf in large heavy-based pot; cook, stirring, until fragrant. Add onion and apple; cook, stirring, until onion softens. Add cabbage, vinegar and the water; cook, covered, over low heat, stirring occasionally, 1 hour. Discard thyme and bay leaf.

NUTRITIONAL INFO PER SERVING 29g total fat (12g saturated fat); 36g carbohydrate; 64g protein; 11g fiber; 678 calories

cassoulet

preparation time 40 minutes (plus standing time) **cooking time** 2 hours 10 minutes **serves** 6

Any white bean such as Great Northern, cannellini or navy beans can be used in this recipe.

1 ½ cups dried white beans

8 ounces boneless pork, sliced thinly

5 ounces bacon, cut into ½-inch pieces

1 ¾ pounds lamb shoulder, diced into
   1 ¼-inch pieces

1 large onion, chopped finely

1 small leek, sliced thinly

2 cloves garlic, crushed

3 sprigs fresh thyme

14 ½-ounce can crushed tomatoes,
   undrained

2 bay leaves

1 cup water

1 cup chicken stock

2 cups dried breadcrumbs

⅓ cup coarsely chopped fresh
   flat-leaf parsley

1 Place beans in medium bowl, cover with water; soak overnight, drain. Rinse under cold water; drain. Place beans in medium pot of boiling water; bring to a boil. Reduce heat; simmer, covered, about 15 minutes or until beans are just tender. Drain.

2 Preheat oven to 325°F.

3 Cook pork in large ovenproof skillet over medium heat, pressing down with back of spoon on pork until browned all over; remove from skillet. Cook bacon in same skillet, stirring, until crisp; remove from skillet. Cook lamb, in batches, in same skillet, until browned all over.

4 Cook onion, leek and garlic in same skillet, stirring, until onion softens. Add thyme, tomatoes, bay leaves, the water, stock, beans and meat; bring to a boil. Cover, transfer to oven; cook 45 minutes. Remove from oven; sprinkle with combined breadcrumbs and parsley. Return to oven; cook, uncovered, about 45 minutes or until liquid is nearly absorbed and beans are tender.

NUTRITIONAL INFO PER SERVING 30g total fat (11g saturated fat); 40g carbohydrate; 57g protein; 12g fiber; 684 calories

pork loin with fresh peach chutney

preparation time 35 minutes **cooking time** 3 hours **serves** 6

4 ½-pound pork loin roast
1 ½ tablespoons olive oil
½ teaspoon celery seeds
1 teaspoon sea salt

Fresh peach chutney
2 large peaches, chopped coarsely
1 large onion, chopped coarsely
¼ cup coarsely chopped raisins
1 teaspoon grated fresh ginger
1 cup sugar
1 cup apple cider vinegar
1 cinnamon stick
¼ teaspoon ground cloves

1 Make fresh peach chutney.

2 Preheat oven to 425°F.

3 Rub pork with half of the oil; sprinkle with seeds. Place pork on wire rack in large baking dish; roast, uncovered, about 1 hour or until juices run clear when pierced with skewer. Remove from oven; place pork on cutting board, cover to keep warm.

4 Increase oven temperature to 475°F.

5 Serve thickly sliced pork with peach chutney. Accompany with a fresh salad of your choice.

Fresh peach chutney Combine ingredients in medium pot, stir over medium heat, without boiling, until sugar dissolves; bring to a boil. Reduce heat; simmer, uncovered, stirring occasionally, about 1 ¾ hours or until mixture thickens.

Tip The chutney can be made up to a week ahead. Place in a sterilized jar while still hot; seal, cool and refrigerate until needed.

NUTRITIONAL INFO PER SERVING 9g total fat (2g saturated fat); 47g carbohydrate; 77g protein; 2g fiber; 581 calories

Italian braised pork

preparation time 25 minutes **cooking time** 2 hours 50 minutes **serves** 6

3 tablespoons olive oil

3 ⅓ pounds pork shoulder, rolled and tied

2 cloves garlic, crushed

1 medium onion, chopped coarsely

½ small fennel bulb, chopped coarsely

8 slices pancetta (4 ounces),
   chopped coarsely

1 ½ tablespoons tomato paste

½ cup dry white wine

14 ½-ounce can whole tomatoes,
   undrained

1 cup chicken stock

1 cup water

2 sprigs fresh rosemary

2 large fennel bulbs (about 2 pounds),
   halved, sliced thickly

Spice rub

1 teaspoon fennel seeds

2 teaspoons dried oregano

½ teaspoon cayenne pepper

1½ tablespoons cracked black pepper

1½ tablespoons sea salt or kosher salt

2 teaspoons olive oil

1 Preheat oven to 350°F.

2 Heat oil in large ovenproof skillet; cook pork, uncovered, until browned all over.

3 Make spice rub.

4 Remove pork from skillet; discard all but 1 ½ tablespoons of the oil in skillet. Cook garlic, onion, chopped fennel and pancetta in same dish, stirring, until onion softens. Add tomato paste; cook, stirring, 2 minutes.

5 Rub pork with spice rub.

6 Return pork to skillet with the wine, tomatoes, stock, water and rosemary; bring to a boil. Cover; transfer to oven, cook 1 hour.

7 Add sliced fennel; cook, covered, 1 hour. Remove pork from skillet. Cover to keep warm.

8 Cook braising liquid in dish over medium heat, uncovered, until thickened slightly. Return sliced pork to skillet; serve pork and sauce with warm Italian bread, if desired.

Spice rub Combine ingredients in small bowl.

Tip Pancetta is an Italian bacon that is cured but not smoked. If you can't find it, substitute prosciutto or bacon.

NUTRITIONAL INFO PER SERVING 33g total fat (11g saturated fat); 8g carbohydrate; 67g protein; 5g fiber; 604 calories

pork loin with spinach and pancetta stuffing

preparation time 30 minutes **cooking time** 1 hour 30 minutes **serves** 8

Ask your butcher to butterfly the pork if possible. This recipe will serve between eight and 12 people depending on your menu.

4 slices white bread

3 tablespoons olive oil

1 clove garlic, crushed

1 medium onion, chopped coarsely

6 slices pancetta, chopped coarsely

3 ½ cups baby spinach

¼ cup toasted macadamias,
    chopped coarsely

½ cup chicken stock

4 ½-pound butterflied pork loin roast

Cherry and red wine sauce

1 ½ cups cherry jam

3 tablespoons dry red wine

⅔ cup chicken stock

1 Preheat oven to 400°F.

2 Cut bread into ½-inch cubes. Heat half of the oil in large skillet; cook bread, stirring, until browned and crisp. Drain croutons on paper towels.

3 Heat remaining oil in same skillet; cook garlic, onion and pancetta until onion browns lightly. Stir in spinach; remove from heat. Gently stir in croutons, nuts and stock.

4 If pork has not been butterflied, place pork on cutting board, fat-side down; slice through thickest part of pork horizontally, without cutting through other side. Open out pork to form one large piece; press stuffing mixture against loin along width of pork. Roll pork to enclose stuffing, securing with kitchen string at one-inch intervals.

5 Place rolled pork on rack in large shallow baking dish. Roast, uncovered, about 1 ¼ hours or until cooked through.

6 Make cherry and red wine sauce.

7 Serve sliced pork with sauce.

Cherry and red wine sauce Combine ingredients in small pot; bring to a boil. Reduce heat; simmer, uncovered, about 10 minutes or until sauce thickens slightly.

NUTRITIONAL INFO PER SERVING 30g total fat (9g saturated fat); 48g carbohydrate; 58g protein; 2g fiber; 702 calories

pork and chicken lettuce leaf wraps

preparation time 20 minutes **cooking time** 45 minutes **serves** 4

Sang choy bow is the term for these delicious lettuce wraps in many Chinese restaurants; the cool lettuce is filled with savory seasoned diced meat.

1 pound boneless pork chops

⅓ cup hoisin sauce

1 ½ tablespoons peanut oil

12 ounces ground chicken

1 clove garlic, crushed

3 ½ ounces fresh shiitake mushrooms, chopped finely

6-ounce can water chestnuts, rinsed, drained, chopped finely

2 green onions, chopped finely

3 tablespoons oyster sauce

1 ½ tablespoons soy sauce

1 teaspoon sesame oil

1 ½ cups bean sprouts

8 large iceberg lettuce leaves

2 green onions, sliced thinly

1 Preheat oven to 350°F.

2 Place pork chops on wire rack in large shallow baking dish; brush all over with ¼ cup of the hoisin sauce. Roast, uncovered, about 40 minutes or until cooked as desired, brushing occasionally with pan drippings. Cool 10 minutes; chop pork finely.

3 Heat peanut oil in wok or skillet; stir-fry chicken, garlic and mushrooms for 5 minutes. Add water chestnuts, chopped onions, oyster and soy sauces, sesame oil, pork and remaining barbecue sauce; stir-fry until chicken is cooked through. Remove from heat; add sprouts, toss mixture gently to combine.

4 Divide lettuce leaves among serving plates; spoon pork mixture into leaves, sprinkle each with sliced onion.

Tip An easy way to remove whole lettuce leaves is to very firmly hit the head, stem-end down, on a hard surface to loosen the core. Discard the core and run a strong stream of cold water into the cavity—the leaves will fall away, intact. Submerge the leaves in iced water until ready to serve.

NUTRITIONAL INFO PER SERVING 13g total fat (3g saturated fat); 18g carbohydrate; 38g protein; 6g fiber; 342 calories

pork green curry

preparation time 15 minutes **cooking time** 25 minutes **serves** 4

1 ½ pounds ground pork

1-inch piece fresh ginger, grated

1 Thai chili, chopped finely

2 cloves garlic, crushed

¼ cup coarsely chopped fresh cilantro

1 tablespoon peanut oil

¼ cup green curry paste

two 14 ½-ounce cans coconut milk

2 tablespoons fresh lime juice

1 tablespoon fish sauce

1 tablespoon grated palm sugar or
  brown sugar

6 ounces green beans, cut into
  2-inch lengths

⅓ cup loosely packed basil or
  Thai basil leaves

1 Combine pork, ginger, chili, garlic and 2 tablespoons cilantro in medium bowl; roll level tablespoons of mixture into balls. Heat oil in large skillet; cook meatballs, in batches, until browned.

2 Add curry paste to same skillet, stirring until fragrant. Add coconut milk; bring to a boil. Reduce heat; simmer, uncovered, stirring occasionally, about 10 minutes.

3 Return meatballs to skillet with lime juice, fish sauce, sugar, and beans; simmer, covered, about 5 minutes or until meatballs are cooked through. Remove from heat; stir in remaining 2 tablespoons cilantro and basil. Serve curry with steamed rice.

NUTRITIONAL INFO PER SERVING 66g total fat (43g saturated fat); 14g carbohydrate; 47g protein; 7g fiber; 845 calories

pork chops with apple fennel relish

preparation time 20 minutes **cooking time** 40 minutes **serves** 4

2 tablespoons cider vinegar
¼ cup olive oil
1 tablespoon Dijon mustard
2 teaspoons sugar
four 8-ounce pork chops

Apple fennel relish
1 large unpeeled Granny Smith apple,
   chopped finely
1 small red onion, chopped finely
1 medium fennel bulb, trimmed and
   chopped finely

Smashed potatoes
2 pounds unpeeled baby red or
   Yukon Gold potatoes
½ cup sour cream
2 tablespoons softened butter
2 tablespoons coarsely chopped fresh dill
¼ cup coarsely chopped fresh
   flat-leaf parsley

1 Whisk together vinegar, oil, mustard, and sugar in medium bowl; transfer
2 tablespoons of dressing to large bowl. Place pork in large bowl; turn to coat.
2 To make relish, combine apple, onion, and fennel in medium bowl with
remaining dressing.
3 Make smashed potatoes.
4 Cook drained pork on grill pan (or grill) until browned on both sides and cooked
to desired degree of doneness, basting with dressing occasionally. Serve pork with
relish and smashed potatoes.

Smashed potatoes Boil, steam, or microwave potatoes until tender; drain. Mash
half the potatoes with sour cream and softened butter in large bowl until smooth;
stir in dill and flat-leaf parsley. Using back of fork, roughly crush remaining potatoes
until skins burst and flesh is just crushed; stir into smooth potatoes.

NUTRITIONAL INFO PER SERVING 52g total fat (22g saturated fat);
44g carbohydrate; 39g protein; 7g fiber; 812 calories

twice-cooked pork

preparation time 15 minutes **cooking time** 1 hour 10 minutes (plus cooling and standing time) **serves** 4

1 ¾ pounds pork belly, skin removed

1 ½-inch piece fresh ginger, grated

2 green onions, chopped coarsely

1 ½ tablespoons vegetable oil

1 medium red bell pepper, sliced thinly

1 medium green bell pepper, sliced thinly

1 medium yellow bell pepper, sliced thinly

2 cloves garlic, crushed

¼ cup hoisin sauce

3 tablespoons dark soy sauce

1 ½ tablespoons lime juice

¼ teaspoon crushed red pepper flakes

3 green onions, sliced thinly

1 Place pork, ginger and chopped onion in wok or skillet; cover with cold water. Bring to a boil then simmer, uncovered, 30 minutes. Cool pork in water; drain.

2 Place pork on baking sheet; let stand about 20 minutes or until completely dried. Slice thinly.

3 Heat oil in cleaned wok or skillet; stir-fry pork, in batches, until crisp. Drain; cover to keep warm.

4 Reserve 2 teaspoons of the oil in wok; discard remainder. Add bell peppers and garlic to wok; stir-fry until tender. Stir in sauces, lime juice and red pepper flakes. Serve bell pepper topped with pork and sprinkled with sliced onions.

Tip "Twice-cooked" Chinese dishes date from days before refrigeration, when people boiled large cuts of meat because it kept better than if left fresh. Here, it also serves the purpose of ridding the meat of some of its excess fat. For extra-crisp pork, serve it on the bell pepper mixture rather than tossing them together.

NUTRITIONAL INFO PER SERVING 50g total fat (16g saturated fat); 11g carbohydrate; 39g protein; 4g fiber; 655 calories

orange-glazed pork chops with spinach and pecan salad

preparation time 20 minutes **cooking time** 20 minutes **serves** 4

½ cup fresh orange juice

¼ cup sugar

2 cloves garlic, crushed

4 pork chops (2 pounds)

Spinach and pecan salad

5 cups baby spinach

¼ cup roasted pecans, chopped coarsely

5 ounces snow peas, trimmed, halved

4 medium oranges (about 2 pounds)

Citrus dressing

3 tablespoons fresh orange juice

1 ½ tablespoons fresh lemon juice

½ teaspoon Dijon mustard

½ teaspoon sugar

2 teaspoons olive oil

1 Combine orange juice, sugar and garlic in small pot, bring to a boil. Reduce heat; simmer, without stirring, about 10 minutes or until glaze reduces to about ⅓ cup.

2 Brush pork chops on both sides with glaze; cook, uncovered, in large, heated, oiled skillet about 10 minutes or until cooked as desired, brushing frequently with remaining glaze. Cover to keep warm.

3 Make spinach and pecan salad.

4 Make citrus dressing. Pour dressing over salad; toss gently to combine. Serve salad with chops.

Spinach and pecan salad Combine spinach, nuts and snow peas in large bowl. Segment peeled oranges over salad to catch juice, add segments to salad; toss gently to combine.

Citrus dressing Whisk together ingredients.

NUTRITIONAL INFO PER SERVING 17g total fat (4g saturated fat); 33g carbohydrate; 44g protein; 6g fiber; 463 calories

roasted pork belly with plum sauce

preparation time 20 minutes **cooking time** 1 hour 55 minutes **serves** 4

1 ¾ pounds boneless pork belly

2 teaspoons salt

1 teaspoon olive oil

1 cup water

1 ½ cups chicken stock

3 tablespoons soy sauce

¼ cup Chinese cooking wine
(or dry white wine)

¼ cup firmly packed brown sugar

2 cloves garlic, sliced thinly

1 ¼-inch piece fresh ginger, sliced thinly

1 cinnamon stick, crushed

1 teaspoon crushed red pepper flakes

⅓ cup fresh orange juice

6 whole cloves

1 teaspoon fennel seeds

4 plums (about 1 pound), cut into
eight wedges

Cucumber salad

1 small cucumber

1 Thai chili or jalapeño pepper, sliced thinly

⅔ cup coarsely chopped fresh mint

1 ½ tablespoons olive oil

1 ½ tablespoons fresh lemon juice

1 teaspoon sugar

1 Preheat oven to 350°F.

2 Place pork on cutting board, fat-side up. Using sharp knife, score fat by making shallow cuts diagonally in both directions at 1 ¼-inch intervals; rub combined salt and oil into cuts.

3 Combine the water, stock, soy sauce, wine, sugar, garlic, ginger, cinnamon, red pepper flakes, orange juice, cloves and fennel in large shallow baking dish. Place pork in dish, fat-side up; roast, uncovered, 1 hour 20 minutes.

4 Increase oven temperature to 475°F. Roast pork, uncovered, additional 15 minutes or until crackling is crisp. Remove pork from dish; cover to keep warm.

5 Strain liquid from baking dish into medium pot, skim away surface fat; bring to a boil. Add plums, reduce heat; simmer, uncovered, about 15 minutes or until plum sauce thickens.

6 Make cucumber salad.

7 Serve thickly sliced pork with plum sauce and salad.

Cucumber salad Using vegetable peeler, cut cucumber lengthwise into ribbons. Place cucumber in large bowl with remaining ingredients; toss gently to combine.

NUTRITIONAL INFO PER SERVING 51g total fat (16g saturated fat); 26g carbohydrate; 39g protein; 3g fiber; 720 calories

roast pork with pear apricot relish

preparation time 10 minutes **cooking time** 20 minutes **serves** 4

14 ½-ounce can sliced pears in
   natural juice
14 ½-ounce can apricot halves in
   natural juice
1 ¼-pound pork tenderloin
1 tablespoon olive oil
½ cup water
2 tablespoons white vinegar
1 fresh small Thai chili, chopped finely
¼ cup golden raisins
2 tablespoons granulated sugar

1 Preheat oven to 475°F.

2 Drain pears over small bowl, reserving juice; coarsely chop pears. Drain apricots, discarding juice; coarsely chop apricots.

3 Place pork in oiled baking dish; drizzle with oil. Roast, uncovered, 20 minutes or until cooked to desired degree of doneness. Cover; let stand 5 minutes and slice into thick pieces.

4 Combine pear, apricot, reserved pear juice and remaining ingredients in medium pot; bring to a boil. Reduce heat; simmer, uncovered, about 20 minutes or until relish thickens slightly.

5 Top pork with relish. Serve with steamed snow peas, if desired.

NUTRITIONAL INFO PER SERVING 8g total fat (2g saturated fat); 29g carbohydrate; 34g protein; 3g fiber; 335 calories

Lamb

Sweet, delicious lamb—once you become an convert to lamb, you'll never look back. Lamb is at its best when served pink in the center.

cardamom-crusted lamb chops with risotto Milanese

preparation time 15 minutes **cooking time** 40 minutes **serves** 4

¼ cup all-purpose flour

1 egg

1 cup dried breadcrumbs

1 teaspoon finely grated lemon peel

1 tablespoon ground cardamom

½ cup finely chopped fresh
  flat-leaf parsley

16 Frenched lamb chops (1 ¾ pounds)

3 cups chicken stock

2 cups water

6 tablespoons olive oil

1 clove garlic, crushed

1 medium yellow onion, chopped coarsely

1 ¼ cups arborio rice

pinch of saffron threads

¼ cup dry white wine

3 ounces baby spinach

1 tablespoon butter

1 Place flour in small shallow bowl; whisk egg in separate small shallow bowl. Combine breadcrumbs, lemon peel, cardamom, and parsley in separate medium shallow bowl. Coat chops, one at a time, in flour then egg then breadcrumb mixture. Place chops, in single layer, on baking sheet; cover, and refrigerate until required.

2 Bring stock and the water to a boil in medium pot. Reduce heat; simmer, covered. Heat 2 tablespoons oil in large pot; cook garlic and onion, stirring, until onion softens. Add rice and saffron; stir rice to coat in mixture. Add wine; bring to a boil. Reduce heat; simmer, stirring, 2 minutes. Stir in 1 cup of the simmering stock mixture; cook, stirring, over low heat, until liquid is absorbed. Continue adding stock mixture, one cup at a time, stirring until liquid is absorbed after each addition. Total cooking time should be about 35 minutes or until rice is just tender. Stir spinach and butter into risotto just before serving.

3 When risotto is almost cooked, heat remaining ¼ cup oil in large skillet; cook chops, in batches, until browned on both sides and cooked to desired degree of doneness. Serve chops with risotto.

NUTRITIONAL INFO PER SERVING 47g total fat (15g saturated fat); 71g carbohydrate; 33g protein; 3g fiber; 846 calories

Greek lamb with skordalia and roasted potatoes

preparation time 40 minutes (plus refrigeration time) **cooking time** 4 hours 20 minutes **serves** 4

Skordalia is a classic Greek accompaniment to meat, made from either potatoes or bread pureed with garlic, olive oil, lemon juice, herbs and, occasionally, ground nuts.

4 ½ pounds leg of lamb (with bone)

2 cloves garlic, crushed

½ cup fresh lemon juice

3 tablespoons olive oil

1 ½ tablespoons fresh oregano

1 teaspoon fresh thyme

1 pinch grated lemon peel

5 large potatoes (about 3 ½ pounds), cut into 1 ¼-inch pieces

3 tablespoons olive oil, extra

1 ½ tablespoons finely grated lemon peel

3 tablespoons lemon juice

1 teaspoon fresh thyme

Skordalia

1 medium potato, quartered

3 cloves garlic, quartered

1 ½ tablespoons lemon juice

1 ½ tablespoons white wine vinegar

3 tablespoons water

⅓ cup olive oil

1 ½ tablespoons warm water

1 Combine lamb with garlic, lemon juice, oil, oregano, thyme and lemon peel in large bowl. Cover; refrigerate 3 hours or overnight.

2 Preheat oven to 325°F.

3 Place lamb in large baking dish; roast, uncovered, 4 hours.

4 Make skordalia.

5 Toss potatoes in large bowl with combined remaining ingredients; place, in single layer, on baking sheet. Roast potatoes, uncovered, for last 30 minutes of lamb cooking time.

6 Remove lamb from oven; cover to keep warm.

7 Increase oven temperature to 425°F; roast potatoes, uncovered, further 20 minutes or until crisp and tender.

8 Serve potatoes and lamb with skordalia; sprinkle with extra fresh lemon thyme leaves, if desired.

Skordalia Boil, steam or microwave potato until tender; drain. Push potato through food mill or fine sieve into large bowl; cool 10 minutes. Place garlic, lemon juice, vinegar and the water in bowl with potato; stir until well combined. Place potato mixture in blender; with motor running, gradually add oil in a thin, steady stream, blending only until skordalia thickens (do not overmix). Stir in the water.

NUTRITIONAL INFO PER SERVING 57g total fat (14g saturated fat); 52g carbohydrate; 91g protein; 7g fiber; 1090 calories

lamb chops with rosemary and garlic

preparation time 20 minutes **cooking time** 20 minutes **serves** 4

¼ cup fresh rosemary sprigs

12 lamb chops (2 pounds)

3 cloves garlic, crushed

2 tablespoons coarsely grated lemon peel

2 fresh small red serrano or Thai chilies,
   seeded, chopped finely (optional)

¼ cup olive oil

2 cups water

1 cup chicken stock

¾ cup polenta

⅓ cup milk

½ cup finely grated parmesan cheese

4 tablespoons butter, melted

3 tablespoons lemon juice

1 Coarsely chop half of the rosemary. Place lamb and chopped rosemary in large bowl with garlic, half of the lemon peel, chili pepper and oil; toss to coat lamb in rosemary mixture. Cook lamb on heated oiled skillet or grill pan until browned on both sides and cooked to desired degree of doneness.

2 Combine the water and stock in large pot; bring to a boil. Stir in polenta gradually; cook, stirring, about 10 minutes or until mixture thickens. Add milk and cheese; stir until cheese melts.

3 Divide polenta among serving plates; top with lamb. Drizzle with combined butter and lemon juice, then sprinkle with remaining peel and rosemary.

NUTRITIONAL INFO PER SERVING 48g total fat (20g saturated fat); 23g carbohydrate; 31g protein; 2g fiber; 645 calories

rack of lamb with parmesan crust and herb risotto

preparation time 30 minutes **cooking time** 40 minutes **serves** 4

½ cup coarsely chopped fresh
   flat-leaf parsley
1 ½ tablespoons finely grated lemon peel
⅓ cup finely grated parmesan cheese
3 cloves garlic, crushed
1 ½ tablespoons olive oil
2 Frenched lamb racks (1 ¼ pounds)

Herb risotto
3 cups chicken stock
3 cups water
1 ½ tablespoons olive oil
1 medium onion, chopped coarsely
1 ½ cups arborio rice
½ cup dry white wine
1 teaspoon finely grated lemon peel
1 fresh small red serrano or Thai chili,
   chopped finely (optional)
½ cup finely grated parmesan cheese
2 cups loosely packed fresh flat-leaf
   parsley leaves

1 Preheat oven to 400°F.
2 Combine parsley, lemon peel, cheese, garlic and oil in small bowl. Place lamb in large shallow oiled baking dish; press cheese mixture onto fatty side of each rack. Roast, uncovered, about 30 minutes or until lamb is cooked to desired degree of doneness.
3 Make herb risotto.
4 Cut each lamb rack in half. Serve with risotto.

Herb risotto Combine stock and the water in medium pot; bring to a boil. Reduce heat; simmer, covered. Heat oil in large pot; cook onion, stirring, about 5 minutes or until onion softens. Add rice; stir to coat in mixture. Add wine; cook, stirring, until liquid is absorbed. Stir in 1 cup simmering stock mixture; cook, stirring, over low heat until liquid is absorbed. Continue adding stock mixture, one cup at a time, stirring, until liquid is almost absorbed after each addition. Total cooking time should be about 35 minutes or until rice is tender. Stir lemon peel, chili pepper, cheese and parsley into risotto just before serving.

NUTRITIONAL INFO PER SERVING 29g total fat (11g saturated fat); 63g carbohydrate; 30g protein; 3g fiber; 649 calories

lamb shanks with five-spice ginger glaze

preparation time 20 minutes **cooking time** 2 hours 10 minutes **serves** 4

Tamarind is an Indian condiment that can be found in Asian or Middle Eastern markets.

2 teaspoons Chinese five spice

1 teaspoon crushed red pepper flakes

1 cinnamon stick

2 star anise

¼ cup soy sauce

½ cup Chinese rice wine or dry white wine

2 tablespoons tamarind concentrate

2 tablespoons brown sugar

3-inch piece fresh ginger, grated

2 cloves garlic, chopped coarsely

1 ¼ cups water

3 ½ pounds lamb shanks

1 pound bok choy, cut into 4-inch lengths

5 ounces sugar snap peas, trimmed

1 Preheat oven to 350°F.

2 Cook five spice, red pepper flakes, cinnamon, and star anise in a dry skillet, stirring, until fragrant. Combine spice mixture with soy sauce, rice wine, tamarind, sugar, ginger, garlic and the water in medium bowl.

3 Place lamb shanks, in single layer, in large shallow baking dish; drizzle with spice mixture. Roast, uncovered, turning shanks occasionally, about 2 hours or until meat is almost falling off the bone. Remove racks from dish; cover to keep warm. Skim away excess fat; strain sauce into small pot.

4 Boil, steam or microwave bok choy and peas, separately, until tender; drain.

5 Divide vegetables among serving plates; serve with lamb racks, drizzled with reheated sauce.

NUTRITIONAL INFO PER SERVING 20g total fat (9g saturated fat); 13g carbohydrate; 48g protein; 3g fiber; 451 calories

lamb shank stew with creamy mashed potatoes

preparation time 20 minutes **cooking time** 3 hours 20 minutes **serves** 8

8 lamb shanks (3 ½ pounds)

8 cloves garlic, halved

2 medium lemons

3 tablespoons olive oil

3 large onions (about 1 ¼ pounds),
   chopped coarsely

2 cups dry red wine

4 large carrots, quartered lengthwise

3 celery stalks, chopped coarsely

4 bay leaves

8 sprigs fresh thyme

1 ¾ quarts (7 cups) chicken stock

½ cup finely chopped fresh flat-leaf parsley

¼ cup finely chopped fresh mint

4 ½ pounds potatoes, chopped coarsely

1 ½ cups heavy cream

7 tablespoons butter

1 Pierce meatiest part of each shank in two places with sharp knife; press garlic into cuts.

2 Grate peel of both lemons finely; reserve. Halve lemons; rub cut sides all over shanks. Preheat oven to 350°F.

3 Heat oil in large ovenproof skillet or Dutch oven; cook shanks, in batches, until browned. In same pan, cook onions, stirring, until softened. Add wine; bring to a boil, then remove pan from heat.

4 Place carrots, celery and shanks, in alternate layers, on onion mixture. Top with bay leaves and thyme; carefully pour stock over the top. Cover dish tightly with lid or aluminum foil; bake about 3 hours or until meat is tender. (Can be made ahead to this stage. Cover; refrigerate overnight.)

5 Combine reserved grated lemon peel, parsley and mint in small bowl.

6 Boil, steam or microwave potatoes until tender; drain. Mash potatoes with warmed cream and butter in large bowl until smooth. Cover to keep warm.

7 Transfer shanks to platter; cover to keep warm. Strain pan juices through cheesecloth-lined sieve or colander into medium pot; discard solids. Boil pan juices, uncovered, stirring occasionally, until reduced by half.

8 Divide mashed potatoes among serving plates; top with shanks, sprinkle with lemon-herb mixture, drizzle with pan juices. Serve with steamed green beans, if desired.

NUTRITIONAL INFO PER SERVING 40g total fat (22g saturated fat); 38g carbohydrate; 39g protein; 8g fiber; 724 calories

Italian shepherd's pie

preparation time 25 minutes **cooking time** 1 hour **serves** 6

1 tablespoon olive oil

1 medium yellow onion, chopped finely

2 cloves garlic, crushed

8 ounces mushrooms, sliced thinly

1 large carrot, diced into ¼-inch pieces

1 medium eggplant, diced

1 ½ pounds ground lamb

1 tablespoon all-purpose flour

½ cup dry red wine

14 ½-ounce can crushed tomatoes

2 tablespoons tomato paste

1 tablespoon Worcestershire sauce

2 tablespoons finely chopped
  fresh oregano

1 ¾ pounds potatoes, chopped coarsely

1 tablespoon butter

⅓ cup milk, warmed

¼ cup finely grated parmesan cheese

Soft polenta

1 ¼ cups chicken stock

¾ cup milk

½ cup polenta

¼ cup finely grated parmesan cheese

1 Preheat oven to 400°F. Grease 9 x 13-inch casserole dish.

2 Heat oil in large skillet; cook onion, garlic, mushrooms, carrot, and eggplant, stirring, until onion softens. Add lamb; cook, stirring, until browned. Add flour; cook, stirring, 1 minute. Add wine; bring to a boil, stirring. Stir in undrained tomatoes, tomato paste, Worcestershire sauce, and oregano. Reduce heat; simmer, uncovered, about 10 minutes or until mixture thickens slightly.

3 Make soft polenta.

4 Boil, steam or microwave potatoes until tender; drain. Mash potatoes with butter and milk in large bowl until smooth. Using wooden spoon, gently swirl hot polenta mixture into potato mixture.

5 Spoon lamb mixture into dish; top with potato polenta mixture, and sprinkle with ¼ cup of parmesan cheese. Cook, uncovered, about 25 minutes or until cheese browns lightly.

6 Serve with baby arugula salad with balsamic vinaigrette, if desired.

Soft polenta Combine stock and milk in large pot; bring to a boil. Gradually add polenta to stock mixture, stirring constantly. Reduce heat; cook, stirring, about 10 minutes or until polenta thickens. Stir in cheese.

NUTRITIONAL INFO PER SERVING 19g total fat (9g saturated fat); 37g carbohydrate; 38g protein; 7g fiber; 488 calories

lamb kabobs with tomato mint salad

preparation time 20 minutes **cooking time** 15 minutes **serves** 4

Soak 8 bamboo skewers in cold water for at least one hour before use to prevent scorching and splintering.

¼ cup olive oil

2 teaspoons grated lemon peel

¼ cup fresh lemon juice

¼ cup finely chopped fresh oregano

1 ½ pounds lamb leg, cut into
   1-inch pieces

2 medium yellow bell peppers,
   chopped coarsely

1 medium red onion, chopped coarsely

2 large tomatoes, chopped coarsely

¼ cup roasted slivered almonds

1 cup firmly packed fresh mint leaves

1 Whisk together oil, lemon peel, lemon juice and oregano in small bowl.

2 Thread lamb, bell peppers and onion, alternately, on skewers. Place on baking sheet; drizzle with half the dressing.

3 Grill kabobs on grill pan (or grill) or until cooked to desired degree of doneness.

4 Combine tomato, almonds and mint with the remaining dressing in small bowl.

5 Serve kabobs with tomato mint salad, and pita bread, if desired.

NUTRITIONAL INFO PER SERVING 26g total fat (6g saturated fat); 8g carbohydrate; 46g protein; 4g fiber; 458 calories

lamb, feta and spinach phyllo pockets

preparation time 25 minutes **cooking time** 25 minutes **serves** 4

9 ounces fresh spinach leaves

¾ cup feta cheese, crumbled

1 tablespoon fresh oregano leaves

½ teaspoon cracked black pepper

1 teaspoon grated lemon peel

eight ¼-pound lamb fillets

8 sheets phyllo dough, thawed

vegetable cooking spray

1 Preheat oven to 475°F. Oil baking sheet; line with parchment paper.

2 Boil, steam or microwave spinach until tender; drain. Rinse under cold water; drain well. Coarsely chop spinach; combine in medium bowl with feta, oregano, pepper and lemon peel.

3 Sauté lamb, in batches, in large skillet until browned.

4 Stack 4 phyllo sheets, spraying individual sheets lightly with cooking spray. Cut phyllo stack in half crosswise; cover with a slightly damp tea towel to prevent drying out. Repeat process with remaining 4 phyllo sheets; you will end up 4 phyllo stacks.

5 Uncover 1 phyllo stack; place on board. Center two fillets on stack; top fillets with a quarter of the spinach mixture. Roll stack to enclose filling, folding in sides after first complete turn of roll. Spray pocket with cooking-oil spray; place on baking sheet. Repeat process with remaining 3 phyllo stacks, lamb and spinach.

6 Bake parcels about 15 minutes or until phyllo is lightly browned. Serve with Greek-style yogurt and lemon wedges, if desired.

Tip For an even richer dish, brush phyllo dough with melted butter instead of cooking spray.

NUTRITIONAL INFO PER SERVING 20g total fat (9g saturated fat); 21g carbohydrate; 53g protein; 3g fiber; 476 calories

Turkish herbed lamb pizza

preparation time 45 minutes (plus standing time) **cooking time** 35 minutes **serves** 4

¾ teaspoon dried yeast

1 teaspoon sugar

¾ cup warm water

2 cups all-purpose flour

1 teaspoon salt

cooking-oil spray

1 ¼ pounds ground lamb

1 ½ tablespoons olive oil

1 small onion, chopped finely

1 clove garlic, crushed

½ teaspoon ground cinnamon

1 ½ teaspoons ground allspice

¼ cup pine nuts, chopped coarsely

¼ cup tomato paste

2 medium tomatoes, seeded,
   chopped finely

1 cup chicken stock

3 tablespoons fresh lemon juice

¼ cup finely chopped fresh flat-leaf parsley

¼ cup finely chopped fresh mint

½ cup Greek-style yogurt

3 tablespoons cold water

1 Whisk yeast, sugar and warm water in small bowl; cover, let stand in warm place about 15 minutes or until mixture is frothy.

2 Combine flour and salt in large bowl; stir in yeast mixture, mix to a soft dough. Knead on lightly floured surface about 10 minutes or until smooth and elastic. Place in large oiled bowl, turning dough once to coat in oil. Cover dough; let stand in warm place about 1 hour or until dough is doubled in size.

3 Halve dough; knead each portion until smooth then roll out to oval shape measuring 5- x 14-inches. Place each oval on a lightly oiled baking sheet; spray lightly with cooking-oil spray. Cover; let stand in warm place 30 minutes.

4 Preheat oven to 475°F.

5 Cook lamb in large, hot non-stick skillet, stirring, until cooked through; place in medium bowl.

6 Heat oil in same skillet; cook onion and garlic, stirring, until onion softens. Add spices and nuts; cook, stirring, about 5 minutes or until nuts are just toasted. Return lamb to skillet with tomato paste, tomatoes, stock and lemon juice; cook, stirring, about 5 minutes or until liquid is almost evaporated. Remove skillet from heat; stir in herbs.

7 Spoon lamb mixture over pizza crusts; bake, uncovered, 15 minutes or until crusts are cooked through and tops are browned lightly. Serve drizzled with combined yogurt and cold water.

Tip You can substitute pre-made pizza dough for homemade crusts.

NUTRITIONAL INFO PER SERVING 27g total fat (8g saturated fat); 63g carbohydrate; 44g protein; 5g fiber; 671 calories

moussaka

preparation time 40 minutes (plus standing time) **cooking time** 1 hour 30 minutes **serves** 6

2 large eggplants, sliced thinly

1 tablespoon kosher salt

¼ cup olive oil

1 large yellow onion, chopped finely

2 cloves garlic, crushed

2 pounds ground lamb

14 ½-ounce can crushed tomatoes

½ cup dry white wine

1 teaspoon ground cinnamon

¼ cup finely grated parmesan cheese

White sauce

6 tablespoons butter

⅓ cup all-purpose flour

2 cups milk

1 Place eggplant in colander, and sprinkle all over with salt; let stand 30 minutes. Rinse under cold water; drain. Pat dry with paper towels.

2 Heat oil in large skillet; cook eggplant, in batches, until browned on both sides; drain on paper towels.

3 Cook onion and garlic in same skillet, stirring, until onion softens. Add lamb; cook, stirring, until lamb changes color. Stir in undrained tomatoes, wine, and cinnamon; bring to a boil. Reduce heat; simmer, uncovered, about 30 minutes or until liquid has evaporated.

4 Preheat oven to 350°F. Grease a shallow 8-cup rectangular baking dish.

5 Make white sauce.

6 Place one-third of the eggplant in dish, overlapping slices slightly. Spread half of the meat sauce over eggplant. Repeat layering with another third of the eggplant, remaining meat sauce, and remaining eggplant. Spread white sauce over top layer of eggplant; sprinkle with cheese. Cook, uncovered, about 40 minutes or until top browns lightly. Cover moussaka; let stand 10 minutes before serving.

White sauce Melt butter in small pot. Add flour; cook, stirring, until mixture thickens and bubbles. Gradually add milk; stir until mixture boils and thickens.

NUTRITIONAL INFO PER SERVING 37g total fat (17g saturated fat); 18g carbohydrate; 42g protein; 5g fiber; 579 calories

Kashmiri lamb with spicy dal

preparation time 30 minutes (plus standing and refrigeration time) **cooking time** 1 hour 15 minutes **serves** 4

1 cup yellow split peas

1 teaspoon hot paprika

2 teaspoons ground coriander

2 teaspoons ground cumin

¼ cup vegetable oil

1-pound boneless leg of lamb

1 medium yellow onion, chopped finely

2 cloves garlic, crushed

¾-inch piece fresh ginger, grated

½ teaspoon ground turmeric

1 teaspoon garam masala

1 teaspoon chili powder

1 cup canned chickpeas

2 medium tomatoes, chopped coarsely

3 cups water

½ cup coarsely chopped fresh
   cilantro leaves

1 Cover split peas with cold water in large bowl. Soak overnight; rinse, drain.

2 Combine paprika, 1 teaspoon coriander, 1 teaspoon cumin, 1 tablespoon oil, and lamb in large bowl. Cover, and refrigerate 3 hours or overnight.

3 Heat 1 tablespoon oil in large pot; cook onion, garlic, and ginger, stirring, until onion softens. Stir in remaining 1 teaspoon each ground coriander and cumin, turmeric, garam masala, and chili powder; cook, stirring, until fragrant.

4 Add split peas, chickpeas, tomatoes, and 3 cups water; bring to a boil. Reduce heat; simmer, covered, stirring occasionally, about 1 hour or until dal is tender. Remove from heat; stir in fresh cilantro.

5 Heat remaining oil in large skillet; cook lamb, uncovered, until browned and cooked to desired degree of doneness. Cover; stand 10 minutes, then slice thinly. Serve with dal. Top with extra cilantro leaves, if desired.

NUTRITIONAL INFO PER SERVING 23.2g total fat (4.7g saturated fat); 44.5g carbohydrate; 54.2g protein; 12.9g fiber; 628 calories

Desserts

What's a fabulous meal without a sweet finale? Whether it's chocolate, cheesecake, or a caramelized fruit tart, we've collected all the recipes you need to satisfy your sweet tooth.

chocolate soufflé with raspberry coulis

preparation time 15 minutes **cooking time** 20 minutes **serves** 4

1 ½ tablespoons sugar

4 tablespoons butter

1 ½ tablespoons all-purpose flour

7 ounces dark chocolate, melted

2 egg yolks

4 egg whites

¼ cup sugar

Raspberry coulis

5 ounces frozen raspberries, thawed

3 tablespoons sugar

4 cloves

½ cup dry red wine

1 Preheat oven to 400°F. Grease four ¾-cup soufflé dishes. Sprinkle insides of dishes evenly with sugar; shake away excess. Place dishes on baking sheet.

2 Melt butter in medium pan, add flour; cook, stirring, about 2 minutes or until mixture thickens and bubbles. Remove from heat; stir in chocolate and egg yolks. Transfer to large bowl.

3 Beat egg whites in small bowl with electric mixer until soft peaks form. Gradually add ¼ cup sugar, one tablespoon at a time, beating until sugar dissolves between additions. Gently fold egg white mixture into chocolate mixture, in two batches.

4 Divide soufflé mixture among dishes; bake, uncovered, about 15 minutes or until soufflés are puffed.

5 Make raspberry coulis.

6 Serve soufflés with coulis.

Raspberry coulis Combine raspberries and sugar in small pot; cook, without boiling, until sugar dissolves. Add cloves and wine; bring to a boil. Reduce heat; simmer, uncovered, about 5 minutes or until coulis thickens. Strain coulis into serving pitcher.

NUTRITIONAL INFO PER SERVING 28g total fat (16g saturated fat); 64g carbohydrate; 9g protein; 3g fiber; 562 calories

chocolate espresso mousse cake

preparation time 40 minutes (plus refrigeration time) **cooking time** 15 minutes **serves** 12

6 eggs, separated
½ cup powdered sugar
¼ cup cocoa powder
3 tablespoons cornstarch
5 ounces dark chocolate, melted
1 ½ tablespoons water
1 ½ tablespoons instant coffee
1 ½ tablespoons hot water
3 cups heavy cream
1 pound dark chocolate, melted
2 teaspoons cocoa powder

1 Preheat oven to 350°F. Grease shallow jelly roll pan; line bottom with parchment paper.

2 Beat egg yolks and sugar in small bowl with electric mixer until thick and creamy; transfer mixture to large bowl. Fold in combined sifted cocoa and cornstarch, then the 5 ounces of chocolate and water.

3 Beat egg whites in small bowl with electric mixer until soft peaks form. Fold egg whites, in two batches, into chocolate mixture. Spread mixture into pan; bake, uncovered, about 15 minutes. Turn cake onto parchment-paper-lined wire rack to cool.

4 Grease 9-inch springform pan; line sides with parchment paper, extending paper 2 inches above edges of pan. Cut 9-inch-diameter circle from cooled cake; place in pan. Discard remaining cake.

5 Dissolve coffee in the hot water in small cup; cool. Beat cream and coffee mixture in medium bowl with electric mixer until soft peaks form. Fold in cooled pound of melted chocolate.

6 Pour coffee mixture over cake in pan, cover; refrigerate 3 hours or until set.

7 Transfer cake from pan to serving plate; dust with 2 teaspoons of sifted cocoa powder.

NUTRITIONAL INFO PER SERVING 41g total fat (25g saturated fat); 42g carbohydrate; 8g protein; 1g fiber; 563 calories

chocolate macadamia squares

preparation time 15 minutes (plus refrigeration time) **cooking time** 5 minutes **makes** 30

1 stick plus 5 tablespoons butter

⅓ cup honey

⅓ cup hot cocoa mix

¼ cup cocoa powder

1 pound vanilla wafers, chopped finely

½ cup roasted macadamia nuts,
   chopped coarsely

7 ounces dark chocolate

1 Line 8- x 12-inch baking pan with plastic wrap.

2 Combine butter, honey, hot cocoa mix and sifted cocoa powder in medium pot; stir over medium heat until mixture is smooth. Add wafers and nuts; stir to combine.

3 Press mixture into pan, cover; refrigerate until firm.

4 Stir chocolate in medium heatproof bowl over medium pot of simmering water until smooth. Spread chocolate over cookie mixture; refrigerate, uncovered, until firm. Cut into 1 ½-inch x 2-inch pieces to serve.

Tip Macadamia nuts can be replaced with any other variety of nut.

NUTRITIONAL INFO PER PIECE 32g total fat (19g saturated fat); 51g carbohydrate; 5g protein; 2g fiber; 514 calories

caramel brownie sundaes

preparation time 10 minutes **cooking time** 20 minutes **serves** 6

6 tablespoons butter

5 ounces dark chocolate,
   chopped coarsely

¾ cup firmly packed brown sugar

2 eggs, beaten lightly

1 teaspoon vanilla extract

¾ cup all-purpose flour

1 ½ cups vanilla ice cream

3 tablespoons almonds, chopped coarsely

3 tablespoons toffee bits

Caramel sauce

⅔ cup heavy cream

4 tablespoons butter

¾ cup firmly packed brown sugar

1 Preheat oven to 425°F. Grease 6-cup oversize (Texas) muffin pan.

2 Combine butter, chocolate and sugar in medium pot; stir over medium heat until smooth. Stir in egg, vanilla and flour; divide mixture among muffin cups. Cover pan tightly with aluminum foil.

3 Bake brownies about 20 minutes. Remove aluminum foil; let stand 5 minutes.

4 Make caramel sauce.

5 Place brownies on serving plates; top with ice cream, sauce, almonds, and toffee bits.

Caramel sauce Combine ingredients in small pot; stir over medium heat until smooth. Simmer 2 minutes.

Tip Caramel sauce and the chocolate-melting stage for the brownies can be done in a microwave oven.

NUTRITIONAL INFO PER SERVING 47g total fat (28g saturated fat); 86g carbohydrate; 8g protein; 1g fiber; 797 calories

dark chocolate and almond torte

preparation time 20 minutes (plus standing time) **cooking time** 55 minutes **serves** 14

You can make your own almond meal by grinding blanched almonds in a food processor until they reach the consistency of cornmeal.

12 ounces dark chocolate,
    chopped coarsely
2 sticks plus 7 tablespoons unsalted butter
5 eggs, separated
¾ cup sugar
1 cup almond meal
⅔ cup toasted sliced almonds,
    chopped coarsely
⅓ cup coarsely grated dark chocolate
1 cup toffee-covered almonds or
    whole almonds (for garnish)

Dark chocolate ganache
4 ounces dark chocolate, chopped coarsely
⅓ cup heavy cream

1 Preheat oven to 350°F. Grease deep 9-inch round cake pan; line the bottom and side with two layers of parchment paper.
2 Stir chopped chocolate and butter in small pot over low heat until smooth; cool to room temperature.
3 Beat egg yolks and sugar in small bowl with electric mixer until thick and creamy. Transfer to large bowl; fold in chocolate mixture, almond meal, sliced almonds and grated chocolate.
4 Beat egg whites in small bowl with electric mixer until soft peaks form; fold into chocolate mixture, in two batches. Pour mixture into pan.
5 Bake cake, uncovered, about 45 minutes. Let cake stand in pan 15 minutes; turn cake, top-side up, onto wire rack to cool.
6 Make dark chocolate ganache.
7 Spread ganache over cake, decorate cake with almonds; let stand 30 minutes before serving.
Dark chocolate ganache Stir ingredients in small pot over low heat until smooth.

NUTRITIONAL INFO PER SERVING 30g total fat (13g saturated fat); 31g carbohydrate; 8g protein; 2g fiber; 425 calories

chocolate mocha dacquoise napoleon

preparation time 20 minutes (plus refrigeration time) **cooking time** 45 minutes **serves** 12

A classic dacquoise is a layered meringue sandwiched with a butter-cream filling. It is served cold, and pairs well with seasonal berries.

4 egg whites

1 cup sugar

3 tablespoons cocoa powder

7 ounces dark chocolate,
    chopped coarsely

¾ cup heavy cream

2 teaspoons cocoa powder, for dusting

Mocha butter cream

1 ½ tablespoons instant coffee

3 tablespoons boiling water

7 tablespoons unsalted butter

2 ¼ cups powdered sugar

1 Preheat oven to 325°F. Line each of three baking sheets with parchment paper; draw a 10 x 10-inch square on each parchment-paper-lined baking sheet.

2 Beat egg whites in medium bowl with electric mixer until soft peaks form. Gradually add sugar, beating after each addition until sugar dissolves; fold in sifted cocoa.

3 Spread meringue mixture evenly over drawn rectangles; bake, uncovered, about 45 minutes or until meringue is dry. Turn off oven; cool meringues in oven with door ajar.

4 Stir chocolate and cream in small pot over low heat until smooth, transfer to small bowl; refrigerate until firm. Beat chocolate mixture with electric mixer about 20 seconds or until just changed in color.

5 Make mocha butter cream.

6 Place one meringue layer on serving plate; spread with half of the chocolate mixture, then top with half of the butter cream. Top with another meringue layer; spread with remaining chocolate mixture, then with remaining butter cream. Top with last meringue layer, cover; refrigerate 3 hours or overnight. To serve, dust with 2 teaspoons of sifted cocoa powder.

Mocha butter cream Dissolve coffee powder with a boiling water in small bowl; cool 10 minutes. Beat butter in small bowl with electric mixer until pale in color; gradually add sugar, beating until combined. Beat in coffee mixture.

NUTRITIONAL INFO PER SERVING 19g total fat (14g saturated fat); 59g carbohydrate; 3g protein; 1g fiber; 415 calories

white chocolate fondue

preparation time 10 minutes **cooking time** 5 minutes **serves** 4

6 ounces white chocolate,
  chopped coarsely

½ cup heavy cream

1 ½ tablespoons Malibu rum

1 cup strawberries

1 large banana, cut into ½-inch slices

5 ounces fresh pineapple chunks

8 slices almond biscotti or sliced cake

16 marshmallows

1 Combine chocolate and cream in small pot, stir over low heat until smooth; stir in liqueur. Transfer fondue to serving bowl.

2 Place fondue in center of serving plate, surrounded by remaining ingredients.

Tip Try a flavored rum, such as coconut, for a richer flavor.

NUTRITIONAL INFO PER SERVING 13g total fat (8g saturated fat); 26g carbohydrate; 3g protein; 1g fiber; 245 calories

quick chocolate rum mousse

preparation time 10 minutes **cooking time** 5 minutes **serves** 4

A variation on the Italian zabaglione, the rum and chocolate transform this into a dessert of great depth and contrasting flavors. Use a Caribbean rum for this recipe, for its mild smooth taste.

6 egg yolks
⅓ cup sugar
½ cup dark rum, warmed
2 ounces dark chocolate, grated finely

1 Beat egg yolks and sugar in small deep-sided heatproof bowl with electric mixer until light and fluffy.
2 Place bowl over small pot of simmering water; whisk egg mixture constantly while gradually adding rum. Continue to whisk until mixture is thick and creamy. Add chocolate, in two batches, whisking until chocolate melts between additions.
3 Pour mousse mixture into four ⅓-cup serving glasses.

Tip The mousse can be served chilled if desired; refrigerate about 2 hours.

NUTRITIONAL INFO PER SERVING 13g total fat (5g saturated fat); 26g carbohydrate; 6g protein; 0g fiber; 302 calories

no-bake cookies-and-cream cheesecake

preparation time 20 minutes (plus refrigeration time) **cooking time** 5 minutes **serves** 12

8 ounces plain chocolate cookies

1 stick plus 2 tablespoons butter, melted

2 teaspoons plain gelatin

¼ cup water

1 ½ cups cream cheese, softened

1 ½ cups heavy cream

1 teaspoon vanilla extract

½ cup sugar

6 ounces white chocolate, melted

5 ounces Oreos or other cream-filled
   chocolate cookies, quartered

2 ounces dark chocolate, melted

1 Line base of 9-inch springform pan with parchment paper.

2 Crush or process plain chocolate cookies until mixture resembles fine breadcrumbs. Add butter; process until just combined. Press cookie mixture by hand over base and 1 ¼ inches up sides of pan, cover; refrigerate 20 minutes.

3 Dissolve gelatin into the water in small heatproof cup; place cup in small pot of simmering water. Stir until gelatin dissolves; cool 5 minutes.

4 Beat cream cheese, cream, vanilla and sugar in medium bowl with electric mixer until smooth. Stir in gelatin mixture and white chocolate; fold in quartered cookies. Pour cheesecake mixture over cookie mixture in pan, cover; refrigerate about 3 hours or until set. Drizzle with dark chocolate to serve.

Tip Place the dark chocolate in a small plastic bag with the corner snipped off to help you drizzle the chocolate evenly over the cheesecake.

NUTRITIONAL INFO PER SERVING 42g total fat (27g saturated fat); 43g carbohydrate; 7g protein; 1g fiber; 574 calories

chocolate butterscotch tartlets

preparation time 5 minutes **cooking time** 10 minutes (plus refrigeration time) **makes** 12

12 frozen tartlet shells

¼ cup firmly packed brown sugar

1 ½ tablespoons butter

½ cup heavy cream

5 ounces dark chocolate,
   chopped coarsely

3 tablespoons coarsely chopped
   roasted hazelnuts

1 ½ tablespoons cocoa powder

1 Bake tartlet shells according to manufacturer's instructions.

2 Heat combined sugar, butter and ¼ cup of the heavy cream in small pot, stirring until sugar dissolves. Reduce heat; simmer, uncovered, without stirring, for 2 minutes. Cool 5 minutes. Stir in chocolate and remaining cream; refrigerate 10 minutes.

3 Divide mixture among tartlet shells, sprinkle with nuts and sifted cocoa.

NUTRITIONAL INFO PER TARTLET 11g total fat (6g saturated fat); 14g carbohydrate; 2g protein; 1g fiber; 165 calories

tiramisu trifles

preparation time 20 minutes (plus refrigeration time) **serves** 4

1 ½ tablespoons instant coffee

½ cup boiling water

3 tablespoons Kahlua, or coffee-flavored
   liqueur

4 ounces ladyfingers (approximately
   11 cookies)

¾ cup heavy cream

⅓ cup powdered sugar

2 cups mascarpone cheese

⅓ cup marsala wine

2 teaspoons cocoa powder

1 Combine coffee and the water in small bowl; stir until coffee dissolves, then stir in liqueur. Cut ladyfingers in half crosswise.

2 Beat cream, powdered sugar and mascarpone with electric mixer in small bowl until soft peaks form; fold in marsala.

3 Dip half of the ladyfingers in coffee mixture; divide among four 1 ½-cup glasses. Divide half of the mascarpone mixture among glasses; dip remaining ladyfingers in coffee mixture, divide among glasses, top with remaining mascarpone mixture.

4 Dust trifles with sifted cocoa; refrigerate until chilled.

NUTRITIONAL INFO PER SERVING 78g total fat (52g saturated fat); 43g carbohydrate; 10g protein; 1g fiber; 948 calories

pear tarte tatin

preparation time 20 minutes (plus refrigeration time) **cooking time** 1 hour 15 minutes (plus cooling time) **serves** 6

3 large firm pears (about 2 pounds)
6 ½ tablespoons butter, chopped
½ cup firmly packed brown sugar
⅔ cup heavy cream
¼ cup roasted pecans, chopped coarsely
(optional)

Pastry
1 ¼ cups all-purpose flour
⅓ cup powdered sugar
6 ½ tablespoons cold butter, chopped
1 egg yolk
1 ½ tablespoons cold water

1 Peel and core pears; cut lengthwise into quarters.

2 Melt butter with brown sugar in large skillet. Add cream, stirring, until sugar dissolves; bring to a boil. Add pears; reduce heat, simmer, turning occasionally, about 45 minutes or until tender.

3 Make pastry.

4 Preheat oven to 425°F.

5 Place pears, round-side down in circular patter, in deep 9-inch round cake pan; pour caramelized pan juices over pears, sprinkle with nuts, if desired.

6 Roll pastry between sheets of parchment paper until slightly larger than circumference of pan. Remove top paper, turn pastry onto pears. Remove remaining paper; tuck pastry between pears and sides of pan.

7 Bake tart, uncovered about 25 minutes or until pastry is browned lightly. Cool 5 minutes; gently flip tart onto serving plate, serve with cinnamon-scented whipped cream, if desired.

Pastry Blend or process flour, powdered sugar and butter until mixture is crumbly. Add egg yolk and water; process until ingredients just come together. Cover with plastic wrap; refrigerate 30 minutes.

NUTRITIONAL INFO PER SERVING 42g total fat (25g saturated fat); 61g carbohydrate; 5g protein; 4g fiber; 647 calories

caramelized apple tarts

preparation time 10 minutes **cooking time** 20 minutes **serves** 4

4 small apples (about 1 pound)

4 tablespoons butter

¼ cup firmly packed brown sugar

½ teaspoon ground cinnamon

½ cup pecans

¼ cup apple sauce

2 teaspoons lemon juice

1 sheet frozen puff pastry, thawed

1 egg, beaten lightly

1 Peel and core apples; slice thinly. Heat butter, sugar and cinnamon in medium pot over low heat until sugar dissolves; add apple. Cook, stirring occasionally, over low heat, until apples soften. Drain apple mixture over medium bowl; reserve caramel mixture.

2 Blend or process pecans, apple sauce and lemon juice until smooth.

3 Preheat oven to 400°F. Line baking sheet with parchment paper.

4 Cut eight 4 ½-inch rounds from pastry sheet; place four of the rounds on tray; brush with beaten egg. Using 3 ½-inch cutter, remove centers from four remaining rounds; center pastry rings on top of the 4 ½-inch rounds. Spread pecan mixture in center of rounds; top with apple mixture.

5 Bake tarts, uncovered, about 15 minutes or until golden brown. Serve warm, with heated reserved caramel mixture.

Tip We used Granny Smith apples in this recipe because their firm white flesh retains its shape and readily absorbs the butter and sugar mixture.

NUTRITIONAL INFO PER SERVING 40g total fat (18g saturated fat); 60g carbohydrate; 8g protein; 4g fiber; 636 calories

pear and plum amaretti crumble

preparation time 10 minutes **cooking time** 15 minutes **serves** 4

You can make your own almond meal by grinding blanched almonds in a nut mill or food processor until they reach the consistency of cornmeal.

28-ounce can plums in syrup, drained, halved, pitted

28-ounce can pear halves in natural juice, drained, halved

1 teaspoon ground cardamom

4 ounces amaretti cookies or almond macaroons, crushed

⅓ cup all-purpose flour

⅓ cup almond meal

½ cup slivered almonds

7 tablespoons butter, chopped

1 Preheat oven to 400°F. Grease deep 6-cup ovenproof dish.

2 Combine plums, pears and cardamom in dish; toss gently to combine.

3 Combine crushed cookies, flour, almond meal and nuts in medium bowl. Using fingers, rub butter into mixture, sprinkle evenly over fruit mixture.

4 Bake, uncovered, about 15 minutes or until golden brown.

Tip This dessert can also be made in four individual 1 ½-cup ramekins and baked for 15 minutes.

NUTRITIONAL INFO PER SERVING 43g total fat (20g saturated fat); 57g carbohydrate; 10g protein; 9g fiber; 670 calories

banana toffee upside-down cake

preparation time 15 minutes **cooking time** 55 minutes **serves** 8

1 cup sugar

1 cup water

2 medium bananas, sliced thinly

2 eggs, beaten lightly

⅔ cup vegetable oil

¾ cup firmly packed brown sugar

1 teaspoon vanilla extract

⅔ cup all-purpose flour

⅓ cup self-rising flour

2 teaspoons allspice

1 teaspoon baking soda

1 cup mashed overripe bananas
   (about 2 large)

1 Preheat oven to 350°F. Grease deep 9-inch round cake pan; line bottom with parchment paper.

2 Stir the sugar and water in medium pot over medium heat, without boiling, until sugar dissolves; bring to a boil. Boil, uncovered, without stirring, about 10 minutes or until caramel in color. Pour toffee into prepared cake pan; top with sliced banana.

3 Combine eggs, oil, brown sugar and vanilla in medium bowl. Stir in sifted dry ingredients, then mashed bananas; pour mixture over toffee and bananas.

4 Bake cake, uncovered, about 40 minutes. Turn onto wire rack, peel off parchment paper; turn cake top-side up. Serve cake warm or at room temperature with whipped cream, if desired.

NUTRITIONAL INFO PER SERVING 20g total fat (3g saturated fat); 74g carbohydrate; 5g protein; 2g fiber; 498 calories

roasted nectarine tart

preparation time 40 minutes (plus refrigeration time) **cooking time** 45 minutes **serves** 8

8 nectarines (about 3 ½ pounds), halved,
  pits removed
¼ cup orange juice
½ cup firmly packed brown sugar

Pastry dough
1 ⅔ cups all-purpose flour
⅔ cup powdered sugar
1 stick cold butter, chopped
1 egg yolk
1 ½ tablespoons cold water, approximately

Pastry cream
1 ½ cups heavy cream
1 cup milk
½ cup sugar
1 vanilla bean
3 egg yolks
3 tablespoons cornstarch
6 ½ tablespoons unsalted butter, chopped

1 Grease 8 x 10-inch tart pan with removable base. Make pastry dough.

2 Make pastry cream while pastry crust is cooling.

3 Increase oven temperature to 425°F. Place nectarines, in single layer, in large shallow baking dish; sprinkle with orange juice and sugar. Roast, uncovered, about 20 minutes or until nectarines are soft. Cool.

4 Spoon pastry cream onto pastry crust, cover; refrigerate about 30 minutes or until firm. Top with nectarines.

Pastry dough Blend or process flour, sugar and butter until combined. Add egg yolk and enough of the water to make ingredients just come together. Knead dough on floured surface until smooth. Cover with plastic wrap; refrigerate 30 minutes. Preheat oven to 350°F. Roll dough between sheets of parchment paper until large enough to line tin. Ease dough into tin, press into sides; trim edges. Cover; refrigerate 30 minutes. Cover pastry crust with parchment paper, fill with pie weights, dried beans, or rice; place on baking sheet. Bake, uncovered, 10 minutes. Remove paper and beans; bake, uncovered, about 10 minutes or until crust is browned lightly. Cool.

Pastry cream Combine cream, milk and sugar in medium pot. Split vanilla bean in half lengthwise, scrape seeds into pot, then add pod; bring to a boil. Remove from heat; discard pod. Beat egg yolks in small bowl with electric mixer until thick and creamy; beat in cornstarch. Gradually beat in hot cream mixture. Strain mixture into same cleaned pot; stir over medium heat until mixture boils and thickens. Remove from heat; whisk in butter. Cover surface of custard with plastic wrap; cool to room temperature.

Tip Uncooked rice or dried beans used to weigh down the pastry are not suitable for eating. Use them every time you bake an unfilled crust; store in an airtight jar.

NUTRITIONAL INFO PER SERVING 41g total fat (26g saturated fat); 82g carbohydrate; 9g protein; 5g fiber; 737 calories

profiteroles with warm chocolate sauce

preparation time 45 minutes (plus refrigeration time) **cooking time** 35 minutes **makes** 36

Choux pastry

5 ½ tablespoons butter

¾ cup water

¾ cup all-purpose flour

3 eggs

Pastry cream

2 ¼ cups milk

1 vanilla bean, split

6 egg yolks

⅔ cup sugar

½ cup all-purpose flour

Warm chocolate sauce

3 ½ ounces dark chocolate,
   chopped coarsely

3 tablespoons butter

⅓ cup heavy cream

1 ½ tablespoons orange-flavored liqueur

1 Make choux pastry.

2 Make pastry cream and warm chocolate sauce.

3 Spoon cooled pastry cream into a large resealable plastic bag. Snip ½ inch off corner of bag and pipe cream through cuts into profiteroles. Serve profiteroles drizzled with warm chocolate sauce.

Choux pastry Preheat oven to 400°F. Grease two baking sheets. Combine the butter with the water in medium pot; bring to a boil. Add flour; beat with wooden spoon over medium heat until mixture comes away from bottom and sides of pot and forms a smooth ball. Remove from heat. Beat in eggs, one at a time, until mixture becomes glossy. Drop rounded teaspoons of choux pastry dough 2 inches apart on baking sheets; bake, uncovered, about 7 minutes or until pastries puff. Reduce oven temperature to 350°F; bake, uncovered, about 10 minutes or until browned lightly and crisp. Cut small opening in side of each profiterole; bake, uncovered, about 5 minutes or until profiteroles dry out. Cool to room temperature before filling with pastry cream.

Pastry cream Bring milk and vanilla bean to a boil in medium pot; remove from heat. Let stand 10 minutes; discard vanilla bean. Meanwhile, beat egg yolks and sugar in medium bowl with electric mixer until thick; beat in sifted flour. With motor running at low speed, gradually beat in hot milk mixture. Return custard mixture to same pot; stir over medium heat until mixture boils and thickens. Reduce heat; simmer, stirring, 2 minutes. Remove from heat; transfer to medium bowl. Cover surface with plastic wrap to prevent skin forming; refrigerate until cold.

Warm chocolate sauce Stir chocolate, butter and cream in small pot over low heat until smooth. Stir in liqueur.

Tips Warm chocolate sauce can be made in a microwave oven. You can use any flavored liqueur in this recipe.

NUTRITIONAL INFO PER PROFITEROLE 6g total fat (4g saturated fat); 11g carbohydrate; 2g protein; 1g fiber; 110 calories

ice cream timbales with chocolate peanut sauce

preparation time 25 minutes **cooking time** 5 minutes **serves** 4

1 quart (4 cups) vanilla ice cream, softened

two 2-ounce Snickers bars, chopped finely

two 2-ounce chocolate covered toffee bars
  (such as Skor or Heath), chopped finely

⅔ cup heavy cream

3 ½ ounces dark chocolate,
  chopped coarsely

one 2-ounce Snickers bar, chopped finely

1 Line four 1-cup metal molds with plastic wrap.

2 Place ice cream in large bowl; fold in chocolate bars. Divide mixture among molds. Cover with aluminum foil; freeze about 15 minutes or until firm.

3 Meanwhile, heat cream and chocolate in small pot over low heat, stirring until smooth. Cool 5 minutes, stir in 2-ounce Snickers bar.

4 Turn ice cream timbales onto serving plates; drizzle with sauce.

NUTRITIONAL INFO PER SERVING 56g total fat (37g saturated fat); 93g carbohydrate; 12g protein; 3g fiber; 926 calories

mini lime cheesecakes

preparation time 15 minutes (plus refrigeration time) **serves** 4

7 ounces vanilla wafers

1 stick butter, melted

8 ounces cream cheese, softened

¾ cup sugar

1 ½ tablespoons finely grated lime peel

3 tablespoons fresh lime juice

1 ½ cups heavy cream

1 Grease four 4 ½-inch-round tart pans with removable bases.

2 Blend or process wafers until mixture resembles fine breadcrumbs. Add butter; process until just combined. Press wafer mixture evenly over bases and around sides of tins, cover; refrigerate while preparing filling.

3 Beat cheese, sugar, lime peel and lime juice in small bowl with electric mixer until smooth.

4 Beat cream in small bowl with electric mixer until soft peaks form; fold into cheese mixture. Spoon filling into tart shells, cover; refrigerate 15 minutes.

Tip You can substitute lemon peel and juice for the lime, if desired.

NUTRITIONAL INFO PER SERVING 82g total fat (52g saturated fat); 81g carbohydrate; 10g protein; 1g fiber; 1100 calories

crème brûlée

preparation time 15 minutes (plus refrigeration time) **cooking time** 40 minutes **serves** 6

1 vanilla bean
3 cups heavy cream
6 egg yolks
¼ cup sugar
¼ cup powdered sugar

1 Preheat oven to 350°F. Split vanilla bean in half lengthwise; scrape seeds into medium heatproof bowl. Heat pod and cream in medium pot, without boiling.

2 Add egg yolks and sugar to seeds in bowl; gradually whisk in hot cream mixture. Place bowl over medium pot of simmering water; stir over medium heat about 10 minutes or until custard mixture thickens slightly and coats the back of a spoon. Discard pod.

3 Divide custard among six ½-cup heatproof dishes. Place dishes in large baking dish; pour enough boiling water into baking dish to come halfway up sides of dishes. Bake, uncovered, about 20 minutes or until custards just set. Remove custards from water; cool to room temperature. Cover; refrigerate 3 hours or overnight.

4 Preheat broiler. Place custards in shallow broiler-safe dish filled with ice cubes; sprinkle custards evenly with sifted powdered sugar. Using finger, distribute the sugar over the surface of each custard, pressing in gently; place under hot broiler until tops of crème brûlées are caramelized.

Tip You can also use a small blowtorch to melt then caramelize the powdered sugar. Small blowtorches are available where cookware is sold.

NUTRITIONAL INFO PER SERVING 52g total fat (32g saturated fat); 20g carbohydrate; 6g protein; 0g fiber; 564 calories

cinnamon flan

preparation time 15 minutes (plus standing and refrigeration times) **cooking time** 1 hour **serves** 8

This recipe must be made 24 hours in advance to allow the caramel to set.

1 cup sugar
½ cup water
2 ½ cups milk
1 ½ cups heavy cream
2 cinnamon sticks
2 whole cloves
4 eggs
2 egg yolks
⅓ cup sugar
2 teaspoons vanilla extract

1 Preheat oven to 325°F.

2 Stir sugar and the water in medium heavy pot over medium heat, without boiling, until sugar dissolves; bring to a boil. Reduce heat; simmer, uncovered, without stirring, until syrup is golden brown in color. Pour syrup over bottom of deep 8-inch round cake pan. Place pan in large baking dish.

3 Combine milk, cream and spices in medium pot; bring to a boil. Remove from heat, cover; let stand 15 minutes. Strain milk mixture; discard spices.

4 Whisk eggs, egg yolks, ⅓ cup of sugar and vanilla in medium bowl. Gradually whisk warm milk mixture into egg mixture, strain mixture over caramel layer in pan. Pour enough boiling water into baking dish to come halfway up sides of pan. Bake, uncovered, about 45 minutes or until custard just sets. Remove pan from water; cool. Cover; refrigerate 24 hours.

5 Just before serving, turn flan onto a rimmed serving dish.

NUTRITIONAL INFO PER SERVING 23g total fat (14g saturated fat); 42g carbohydrate; 7g protein; 0g fiber; 404 calories

banana caramel sundaes

preparation time 10 minutes **cooking time** 10 minutes **serves** 6

2 ounces dark chocolate, chopped finely
⅔ cup roasted walnuts, chopped coarsely
1 ¾ pints vanilla ice cream
4 medium bananas, chopped coarsely

Caramel sauce
6 ½ tablespoons butter
½ cup heavy cream
½ cup firmly packed brown sugar

1 Make caramel sauce.
2 Divide one-third of the sauce among six ¾-cup glasses; divide half the chocolate, nuts, ice cream, and bananas among glasses. Repeat layering process, ending with a layer of the sauce.
Caramel sauce Combine ingredients in small pot. Stir over low heat until sugar dissolves; bring to a boil. Reduce heat; simmer, uncovered, 5 minutes. Cool.

NUTRITIONAL INFO PER SERVING 42g total fat (22g saturated fat); 56g carbohydrate; 7g protein; 2g fiber; 617 calories

mille-feuille with raspberries and almonds

preparation time 25 minutes **cooking time** 15 minutes (plus refrigeration and cooling time) **serves** 8

Mille-feuille, pronounced meal-fwee, translates as "thousand leaves," and refers to puff pasty used in multi-layered sweet or savory dishes. We've adapted the classic dessert version here by layering phyllo pastry with almonds and honey.

1 ⅓ cups milk

4 egg yolks

½ cup sugar

3 tablespoons all-purpose flour

1 ½ tablespoons cornstarch

1 teaspoon vanilla extract

4 tablespoons butter

1 ½ tablespoons honey

2 sheets phyllo dough, thawed

⅓ cup roasted blanched almonds,
   chopped finely

¾ cup heavy cream

10 ½ ounces raspberries

1 Bring milk to a boil in medium pot. Combine egg yolks, sugar, flour, cornstarch, and vanilla in medium bowl; gradually whisk in hot milk. Return custard mixture to same pot; stir, over medium heat, until mixture boils and thickens. Return custard to same bowl, cover; refrigerate about 1 hour or until cold.

2 Combine butter and honey in same cleaned pot; stir, over low heat, until smooth.

3 Preheat oven to 400°F. Grease two baking sheets.

4 Brush one phyllo sheet with half of the honey mixture; sprinkle with nuts. Top with remaining phyllo sheet; brush with remaining honey mixture. Cut phyllo stack into 3-inch squares; place squares on baking sheets. Bake, uncovered, about 5 minutes or until browned lightly. Cool 10 minutes.

5 Beat cream in small bowl with electric mixer until soft peaks form; fold into cold custard mixture. Place one pastry square on each serving plate; top each with two tablespoons of the custard mixture and a few raspberries. Place second pastry square on each; repeat with another layer of custard and raspberries then top each with third pastry square. Serve mille-feuilles with remaining raspberries; dust with powdered sugar, if desired.

NUTRITIONAL INFO PER SERVING 22g total fat (11g saturated fat); 28g carbohydrate; 6g protein; 3g fiber; 337 calories

summer berry stack

preparation time 20 minutes **cooking time** 5 minutes **serves** 4

Brioche is a delightfully sweet, buttery bread; if you can't find it at your supermarket, look for it in your local bakery.

1 pound brioche loaf
8 ounces strawberries, sliced thickly
5 ounces raspberries
5 ounces blueberries
1 ½ tablespoons powdered sugar

Blackberry coulis
10 ½ ounces frozen blackberries
¼ cup powdered sugar
¼ cup water

1 Make blackberry coulis.

2 Cut twelve ½-inch-thick slices from brioche loaf; using 3-inch cutter, cut one round from each slice.

3 Combine berries in medium bowl.

4 Place one round on each plate; divide a third of the berries among rounds. Place another round on top of each stack; divide half of the remaining berries among stacks. Place remaining rounds on berry stacks; top with remaining berries.

5 Pour coulis over stacks; dust each with sifted powdered sugar.

Blackberry coulis Stir ingredients in medium pot over high heat; bring to a boil. Reduce heat; simmer, uncovered, 3 minutes. Strain coulis into medium measuring cup; cool 10 minutes.

NUTRITIONAL INFO PER SERVING 7g total fat (3g saturated fat); 55g carbohydrate; 8g protein; 10g fiber; 314 calories

mixed berry baked cheesecake

preparation time 25 minutes (plus refrigeration time)
cooking time 35 minutes **serves** 8

8 ounces plain chocolate cookies
1 stick butter, melted
two 8-ounce packages cream cheese, softened
½ cup sugar
1 ½ tablespoons fresh lemon juice
2 eggs
⅓ cup sour cream
1 ½ tablespoons all-purpose flour
1 ½ cups frozen mixed berries, thawed

1 Grease an 8 x 12-inch baking pan and line with parchment paper.
2 Blend or process cookies until mixture resembles fine breadcrumbs. Add butter; process until just combined. Press cookie mixture into base of pan, cover; refrigerate until firm.
3 Preheat oven to 275°F. Beat cream cheese, sugar and lemon juice in large bowl with electric mixer until smooth. Add eggs, sour cream and flour; beat until combined. Spread cream cheese mixture over cookie base; sprinkle with berries. Bake, uncovered, about 35 minutes. Cool to room temperature; refrigerate until firm.

Tip Use a hot knife to make cutting the cheesecake easier.

NUTRITIONAL INFO PER SERVING 44g total fat (27g saturated fat); 38g carbohydrate; 10g protein; 1g fiber; 588 calories

Index